FREE INTERNET LEGAL RESEARCH

FREE INTERNET LEGAL RESEARCH

Wanita M. Scroggs

Sally G. Waters

VANDEPLAS PUBLISHING, LLC

UNITED STATES OF AMERICA

Free internet legal research

Scroggs, Wanita M. & Waters, Sally G.

Published by:

Vandeplas Publishing, LLC – August 2014

801 International Parkway, 5th Floor
Lake Mary, FL. 32746
USA

www.vandeplaspublishing.com

ISBN 978-1-60042-227-0

For our Bobs and our Arthurs…

Contents

Acknowledgements

The authors wish to express their deepest gratitude and admiration to all those who strive to make information freely accessible... particularly legal information. We recognize that all sorts of people work toward this same goal: those who work in private and government jobs, for profit and not for profit, those who work in the legal profession and those who are engineers in the information industry. This is truly the information age. All of these unsung heroes are creating the tools for today, as well as for tomorrow. None of this information access happens automatically. It happens because of the hard work and dedication of people all around the world, who make a conscious choice to strive for free access to information. And we thank them.

We would specifically like to thank all of those website owners / sponsors who have so graciously allowed us to include screenshots of their products in this book. We want to show you, our readers, all of the great things that are out there for you to use. Showing is always better than just telling. Very special thanks to the following (in no particular order):

Samuel Clay at Newsblur.com;

the wonderful folks at Yahoo.com and Yahoo Finance;

Google.com, Google Advanced Search, and Google Scholar;

Dr. Jabeur Fathally at University of Ottawa and all of the people who work on Juriglobe.ca;

the people who do all of the great work for the U.S. government who bring us LOC.gov, Congress.gov, FDSys, and so much more;

Kenia Escobar and The Florida Bar and all those at bar associations around the U.S.;

The American Bar Association;

the good people at LawSource, Inc. who give us ALSO and special thanks to Brian Vaughn;

Cornell LII, World LII, and all the members of the Free Access to Law Movement;

Municode.com with a special thanks to Steffanie Rasmussen who is so gracious and helpful;

The American Society of International Law which makes available the ERG, Eisil.org, ASIL Insights and so much more, with special thanks to Sheila Ward who answers all of our questions with unfailing good humor and patience;

and all around great guy, Andrew Zimmerman of Zimmerman's Research Guide. Andy, let us just say, we want to be you when we grow up... assuming we ever do grow up.

If we have missed anyone, please forgive us and know that we are thinking of you fondly and so appreciate the work that you do.

Any mistakes in this book are strictly our own, and definitely unintentional. We are happy to be corrected and welcome any comments or suggestions! You may contact us at scroggswaters@gmail.com .

Happy reading!

Table of Figures

.

Introduction

The internet is one of the most powerful tools a lawyer can use, and it becomes more indispensable each day. Legal information that is needed in practice – cases, statutes, regulations, secondary sources, city ordinances, foreign law, international sources – they're there, on your computer, waiting for you to use, and many of them are available totally free. No monthly charge, no download fees, no subscription needed – many sources of law are available on the internet, free.

Of course, this being law that we're talking about, it isn't necessarily easy to find. And that's why we've written this book. Internet sites are constantly being added or changed, and even attorneys familiar with some sites may not know of things only recently made available free on the internet. And that's why we're here.

Who are we? And how do we know all this?

We're two lawyer-librarians who have spent many years helping attorneys with their legal research issues, and teaching law students how to head off into practice with the knowledge of how to do cost-effective legal research. One of us (Sally) has been doing legal research since before the advent of personal computers, since the early 1980s when Lexis used a dial-up modem and the internet would have seemed like something from "The Jetsons". The other (Wanita) still has her original AOL email address from twenty years ago. The grandkids say that is *not cool*! Both of us decided we liked research and teaching and went into legal education instead of practice. Research is what we do each day – and that daily use has ensured that we keep up with the latest developments in research methods and sites. We know where the good stuff is and how to use it; that's what we're going to show you here.

Disclaimer!

We are lawyers. You knew there would be a disclaimer. We intend this book as a reference tool for practicing attorneys. It is ***not*** intended as legal advice. If you are not an attorney and you have a legal issue that you are dealing with, we highly recommend that you hire an attorney. The state bar association can help you locate a licensed attorney in your area. In many cases it can also give you a directory of board certified attorneys in your area.

How to use this book

This book is intended for reference, just one of many tools in your toolbox. We want you to be able to find the sections pertaining to what you need, and then easily find the parts most helpful to you. We know – we expect! – that you probably won't read it all the way through, front to back, marveling at the brilliance of the prose and the plot (there isn't one). This is a book meant for you to use! We've tried to organize it in a way that will make the information you are looking for easily accessible, so that you can go right to what you need. Each chapter will begin with a **Quick Start** page and then go into more detail. If you browse through the table of contents you will see that we tried to arrange the chapters by type of information or document. You can also use the index to (hopefully) go right to a specific item.

Along the way, though, we've tried to include other things that will be helpful to you, and mark those so that they also are easily found. We've included quick tips on using the many sites we point out, and general internet tips that will help you make the most efficient use of your time on the computer. You'll spot **Quick Tip** boxes throughout the text; you'll find many screen shots from the web sites that we point out. If there are websites that we discuss and we don't include screenshots, it is probably because we were not able to secure copyright permission from the website publisher. Please don't think that we like those sites any less than the others. We've also included a "Tips and Tricks" chapter toward the end of the book to include some information to help you become a great internet searcher.

We have included a chapter that covers some sites for information that might be useful to you even though they aren't 'law sites'. Do you find yourself sometimes needing medical or business information? We've covered things like that, as well as free ways to find personal information that might be handy in your practice.

What kind of sites are included here?

We've included in this book web sites that we use on an almost daily basis. Many of the sites that we recommend are excellent for several different kinds of law – e.g., www.lawsource.com is not only terrific for state law, but also for federal law and even some secondary sources. We've evaluated these sites, and found them reliable and full of good, useful information.

One thing to remember, though – just as the law is constantly changing, so are web sites. Web addresses change, site ownership can change, and sometimes sites are just plain inaccessible when you need them! The sites included here should be easily (and freely) accessible; however, if for some reason one doesn't give you the information that you want, others in that same chapter may have what you need.

And one last thing…

Any book about the internet needs to be updated frequently, and we're hoping to do that with this book. Do you have any suggestions about what we should include in the future? Recommendations of sites? All feedback is welcome and very much appreciated; you can write to us at scroggswaters@gmail.com.

And now – off to see the sites!

Chapter 1

Planning Your Research and Evaluating Resources

Quick Start Page

Uniform Electronic Legal Material Act (UELMA)

http://www.uniformlaws.org/Act.aspx?title=Electronic%20Legal%20Material%20Act

At this website you can find the language of the final act, a summary of the act, why states should adopt it, and other legislative information.

Planning your research should include decisions about: jurisdiction, primary or secondary materials, current or historical materials, print or electronic materials, and search terms.

Some factors to consider when evaluating a resource: purpose, authority, scope, currency, audience, format, objectivity, cost, and navigation or search options.

For more on these topics, read on…

Planning Your Research and Evaluating Resources

Every research session should begin with a plan. What is your jurisdiction? Do you need primary or secondary materials? Do you need current or historical materials? Would print or electronic materials be best? What search terms will you use? Once you have planned what you are looking for, next you'll need to evaluate different sources for those items.

In legal research, you first need to determine your jurisdiction. Which jurisdiction are you in and what type of legal system governs there? Decide if you need federal, state, or local materials. If you need state materials, are you in Louisiana? You may be dealing with a civil law situation rather than common law, in which case you may need code (statutes) only, rather than statutes *and* case law. You can read more about the different legal traditions in the chapter on foreign law.

Now that you have decided which jurisdiction you are in, you should decide if you need primary or secondary materials. Primary legal materials are the law itself: statutes, court opinions, administrative regulations. Secondary materials are analysis, commentary, or explanation of the law. While primary materials may be binding in your situation, secondary materials are not. Primary materials may be binding (mandatory) depending on jurisdiction and currency. For example if the case law is from the highest court in your jurisdiction and it has not been overturned, it will be mandatory for you to follow. If it is from a neighboring jurisdiction it will not be binding on you, but could be used persuasively. Secondary material is never mandatory, but can be very useful in helping you learn your way around the law or a specific legal issue. Secondary materials include things like bar journal articles, legal encyclopedias, legal dictionaries, and practice guides. They will explain an area of the law to you, point out anything that may be tricky or unusual in that area, and point you to the primary sources. Because this book is all about free online legal research, of course we will concentrate on the types of secondary sources that are available for free online. See more in the chapter on secondary sources. Just remember that you can use many of these items in print at your local law library.

If you have decided that you need primary sources, now you should decide if you need current or historical versions. This depends on your use of the materials. We all know that it's important to check your sources to be sure they are "still good law". You don't want to rely on a statute that has been repealed or a case that has been overturned. So, other than writing a historical novel, why would you want older primary materials? One example would be, a client comes into your office and is having trouble over something that happened five years ago. You don't need the current statute, you need to see what the statute said five years ago... at the time of the event in question. Wherever possible we will tell you about online sources that have some older materials available. Really old items may not be available online. If they aren't, we'll try to give you some tips on where to find them.

Another consideration in planning your research is whether you want to use print or electronic sources. Obviously, we love the electronic ones… especially if they're free. Unfortunately, they aren't always, in which case a great alternative is to find the print version that *someone else* has already paid for and that you can use for free. This is where your friendly local law library comes in! A good tip is that librarians generally like chocolate (to eat) and cats (to pet)… please don't get those mixed up. However, be sure to find out what *your* librarians like and spoil them as much as possible. Making friends can take you a long way toward reaching all kinds of goals.

The next step is to think about your search terms. If you are not yet familiar with the legal topic you are researching, this is where a secondary source can be really helpful. Not only will you be able to educate yourself about the topic, a good secondary source will also provide the terms of art, or subtopics, that you want to use as your search terms. You may want to make a list of these terms before you start your serious searching. There is nothing quite as frustrating as being in the middle of research, getting few or no search results, and having to stop to regroup and think about your choice of terms. You may even want to keep notes as you research, so you'll remember which terms yielded great results and which ones were duds.

OK. You have your plan in place. You know what jurisdiction you are in and what legal system governs. You know if you need primary materials or secondary or both. You know the time frame that you want. You know if you want to use print or electronic sources and you have chosen your search terms. Now which sources to use? There are a few things to consider when deciding on sources. Some of the factors we'll talk about are: purpose, authority, scope, currency, audience, format, objectivity, cost, and navigation or search options.

Generally you want to match the purpose of your source with your own purpose. For example, you wouldn't want to cite to a novel as support for an argument in court. If you are writing for an academic journal, you could cite to other academic journals. If you're arguing in court, you probably want to stay with current primary sources only (statutes, court opinions that are binding in your jurisdiction, pertinent administrative regulations, etc). If you're teaching the third grade, you may want to use the kids' pages of a particular resource because their purpose is to teach children. Take a minute to think about the purpose of the source that you're using. Normally you can find that information, especially on a webpage, in the About Us section.

Authority is another factor to consider when evaluating a resource. This is something you will probably hear from us throughout the book… go right to the source if you can! Who has authority to write the law that you need? If you can, go right to that law-making body. If it's a municipal ordinance, go to the city government to get the ordinance. You know they have authority to tell you what the law is, because they are the ones who wrote it! If you need a state statute, try the state legislative website. Need a court opinion, try the court itself. This is a great way to be sure of the authority of the source. Otherwise, consider who is presenting the information. Is it an educational institution? These websites end in .edu. Generally, educational institutions are reliable. Is it a government source? Usually (not always) those web addresses end in .gov. Again, if you get the law right from the government entity that wrote it, that is likely to be the best source. We'll talk more about that in the section on the Uniform Electronic Legal Material Act (UELMA). Did you find the information on a .com or .org website? They can be reliable and carry some authority, but beware. Know who they represent before you trust what they provide.

The scope of a resource is something that is useful to know. Scope simply means what is covered. Is this primary sources only or secondary? Is it current only or also historical? What is in here and what is not? Usually a website will have a "scope note" in a section called About Us. Sometimes it will be labelled Who We Are or What We Do. Sometimes it will say About This Website. Somewhere, they should tell you the purpose of the website and what you can expect to find there. If you are in a big database and are looking at individual sources within the database, each source will often have a small button with a question mark in it, or perhaps the letter i (for information). If you click on that button, it will give you the scope note for that particular resource. In case you hadn't noticed, books also have scope notes. Generally they are in the introduction. Hopefully we have done a sufficient job with ours so that you recognize it for what it is.

Each resource should also tell you how current it is. For traditional print materials this is pretty easy to determine. You just look for the copyright date. In a print book you can find the copyright date on the back of the title page. With many print legal materials there will be a supplementary pocket part in the back of the book, or advance sheet at the end of the set of books. These tend to be paperback because they are faster, easier, and cheaper to print and send out than new hardbound volumes. With electronic materials, it can be trickier. Each website should have a copyright date, usually at the bottom of the first (landing) page. However, individual pages of a website may have different copyright dates. If you are relying on an electronic source for professional information, they should tell you exactly how current the information is, how and how often they update, and if they don't give you that information… don't trust them to be current.

Evaluating the intended audience of the resource is sort of related to evaluating the purpose. Is the information you have found intended for legal professionals, self-represented litigants, school aged children? Are you the intended audience? As we will discuss throughout the book, just because a resource is labelled "for the public" or "for paralegals", doesn't mean that lawyers can't use it also! Just be a smart consumer of information and understand for whom the resource is intended.

Format is another factor to consider. Obviously, this book is about online resources. Sometimes print can be easier (and less expensive) to use. If the source you are looking for is a privately published practice guide, the online version may be very expensive. Yet your local law library may own the print version and allow you to use it for free. We will tell you all about online sources (electronic format) in this book. However, keep in mind that they may not be your best option. Sometimes actual old fashioned paper books are easier to use. You will always have to be your own judge. Sometimes we even have to tell ourselves, "step awaaaaay from the computer". If you are comfortable with electronic sources, and you can find good ones that are free or low cost, they may be your format of choice. Hopefully, we will help you get comfortable, and lead you to some good ones... or at least give you strategies to find them for yourself.

Now for a word about objectivity... no resource is objective. Everyone has a unique viewpoint. Just be aware that every person, every source has bias. Think about what that bias is likely to be. Be sure to balance the information that you gather. Obviously .com websites are commercial, so think about who provides the funding. That will be your biggest clue to the bias of the source. Similarly .org websites, for non-profit organizations, are normally created by advocacy groups. Their information will be biased toward advocating for their own special cause. If you are using a government website, it will most likely (and hopefully) be biased in favor of that particular region... United States government websites and the information they present will be biased in favor of the best interests of the U.S., Florida government websites biased in favor of the best interests of the state of Florida, etc. We can hope that our elected representatives will act in our best interest. That is why we elect them. But still, that is a bias. Be cognizant that each source of information has its own lens through which it views the world. Bias is not bad, it just is. It is up to you to be sure you gather information from all perspectives.

Cost. Finally we get to some real life concerns! You're reading this book because you want to know how to save yourself some money. Everything has a cost. Sometimes cost is purely financial. Sometimes the cost is "opportunity cost": the time I spend doing research in this way, is time that I am not able to spend doing something else. The best way to do cost effective legal research is to know the best sources for different situations. A common strategy is to start with free sources. Do as much background research as you can. Get yourself educated about the topic and find what you think are the leading primary sources. Then if necessary use the pay databases to double check that you are all current. We will be the first ones to say that we love Lexis Shepardizing and Westlaw Keyciting... and if they save you time, that is also saving you money. One tip we can offer is that many law libraries now have free (though limited) access to Westlaw. Very often the packages include just the basics of federal and local state law. But that is certainly enough to jump on and KeyCite what you have found through your research. We are currently unaware of a similar program with Lexis, though if that comes about we will be glad to discuss it as well.

Navigation or search options will be discussed throughout the book, as we talk about specific sources. Just like a print resource has multiple ways to find the information that you need, so should electronic sources. An old fashioned print book will contain a Table of Contents, normally in the front, which presents the contents in some logical way. A book should also have an index, normally at the back, which allows you to look for specific terms or subjects. There may be additional tables, of case names, or maybe of illustrations. In the same way, electronic resources should let you search and also browse. A keyword search box lets you type in exactly what you are looking for and go right to it. If you're not sure what you need, a site map or an A-Z index, often found at the bottom of a webpage, will let you browse what is available. We are also big fans of the Advanced Search... you will get tired of us telling you to "check out the advanced search". We will say that every chance we get, throughout the book, and in person. Don't say we didn't warn you! Seriously, an advanced search can save you tons of time. It can present to you ways of searching that may not have occurred to you otherwise. And if you take a couple of seconds to look at the advanced search, but go back to a regular keyword search, no harm has been done.

Chances are you do all of this kind of evaluating subconsciously. We are bombarded with information every day from all sides and we instinctively consider the source. As you can tell, information professionals actually think about these things a lot. We take these criteria pretty seriously. So much so, that we are concerned about the current state of information creation, particularly legal information. More and more primary legal information is created, stored, and accessed digitally. Unfortunately, this is not always done by people who are information professionals or who have considered these issues. Enter UELMA, the Uniform Electronic Legal Material Act.

http://www.uniformlaws.org/Act.aspx?title=Electronic%20Legal%20Material%20Act

UELMA was completed by the Uniform Law Commissioners in 2011. Like all other uniform laws, it must then be adopted by each jurisdiction in order to enter into effect. Individual states may amend before adoption (it includes a choice of alternative provisions), adopt as is, or totally ignore it. Specifically, UELMA addresses the need for official electronic legal material to be authenticated (so that you can be sure it is the real thing and unaltered), preserved, and permanently, publicly accessible. As of this writing, UELMA has been enacted in eight states and introduced into four more plus the District of Columbia. You can find lots more information on the website above, including great reasons why states should adopt UELMA.

Chapter 2

Local Law

Quick Start Page

Municipal Code Corporation – publisher of local codes and ordinances, has a searchable online library.

www.Municode.com

 Another good strategy for finding local codes is to look on the local government's website.

For more on this topic, read on…

Local Law

As we will tell you many times throughout the book, go right to the source if you can. The same holds true for researching local codes and ordinances. If the city or county government has its own website, as many now do, go there first to find the code. This would be the place to find not just the code but other information as well. The local government website should also tell you things like how and when the code is to be amended, how to get involved in that process, and how to report code violations.

Municipal Code Corporation (a.k.a. Municode) is a publisher of many local codes around the United States. You may even find that when you are on a local government website and you click on the link for the code, it will actually take you out on the internet to Municode's online library. We love www.municode.com! (see Figure 2-1)

Figure 2-1

Municode

You are able to browse and search the free library by clicking on the Browse the Library button. You'll be taken to a page with an interactive map of the United States. (see Figure 2-2) You can click on the state that you want or choose it from a pull down menu.

Figure 2-2

Municode

Once on the page for your particular state, you will then be able to choose the city or county that interests you. From within the code then you can browse using the menu on the left or search for particular terms using the search box at the top. (see Figure 2-3) For any

12

source, it is always good to have multiple access points to the same information, like a browse function and a search box. That would be similar to having a table of contents and an index in a traditional print book.

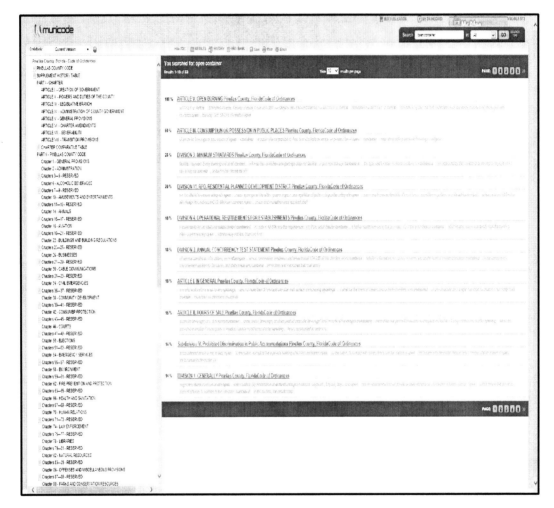

Figure 2-3

Municode

For the more serious consumer of local law, Municode does offer a subscription service, called MuniPro. This service offers things like multijurisdictional searching, the capability to add notes to code sections, and the option to save code sections for faster access. You may also buy a print copy of the codes from Municode. This may be especially helpful if you work for a particular local government and want to have the code close at hand, at times when you may not have internet access. But be aware that the browsable and searchable online library is free of charge and quite helpful for most common local ordinance questions. So, for example, a client comes in with a complaint that the neighbor's dogs are large and vicious looking and constantly running loose in the neighborhood! Jump on Municode.com, navigate to your city or county code, search for the term leash or dog, and voila… your local leash law. Municode will also then give you the contact information, and a link to the website if available, for your local government. You just click or call your local government to report that violation and get some relief for your client.

So, besides the government website and Municode, here are a few other tips for finding local codes or ordinances… you may want to try the local public library in the city or county that interests you. They may have copies of the current code as well as older versions of the code, and other city or county directories, too. Don't forget that there are lots of information junkies out there who may have saved the very piece of information that you need. The local library is a good place to ask, and if they don't have what you need, they will likely know who does. Another great starting place, a website that you will find we have mentioned throughout the book, is American Law Sources Online (ALSO) www.lawsource.com . (see Figure 2-4) ALSO is a wonderful aggregator of free legal resources… not just local, but state, and federal, as well as sources for Mexico and Canada. If you're not sure where to find the good free sources, start with ALSO.

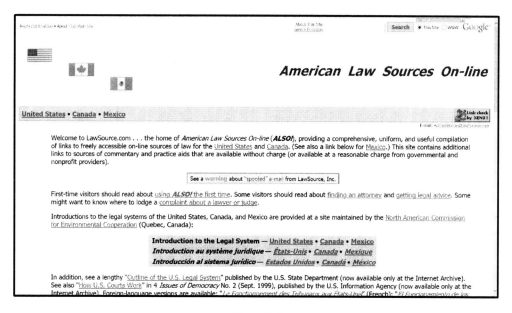

Figure 2-4

Law Source, Inc.

One more search strategy that can be very helpful when searching for local government information… Google Advanced Search. www.google.com/advanced_search

(see Figure 2-5) Google Advanced Search is just like it sounds… advanced search functions using the power of Google. You will find many useful search fields here including one that lets you specify Site or Domain. In this field you could type in .gov if you want search returns only from government websites whose addresses end in .gov. Or you could type in the entire web address of a local government and it will search just that particular website for whatever search terms you enter. This comes in handy when you have found the government website in question, but are not finding the code or ordinance on that website. Let Google search the site for you. Many websites will have a Google search box already installed, but if they don't you can use Google Advanced Search to do it yourself. Google Advanced Search also lets you search by file type. It is frequently helpful when looking for official legal information to limit the file type to .pdf. Many official legal documents are provided in this format. Google will then search for your terms, at the site or domain you have chosen, and only return .pdf documents. Try different combinations of search fields with Google Advanced Search. You may be surprised at how useful this is.

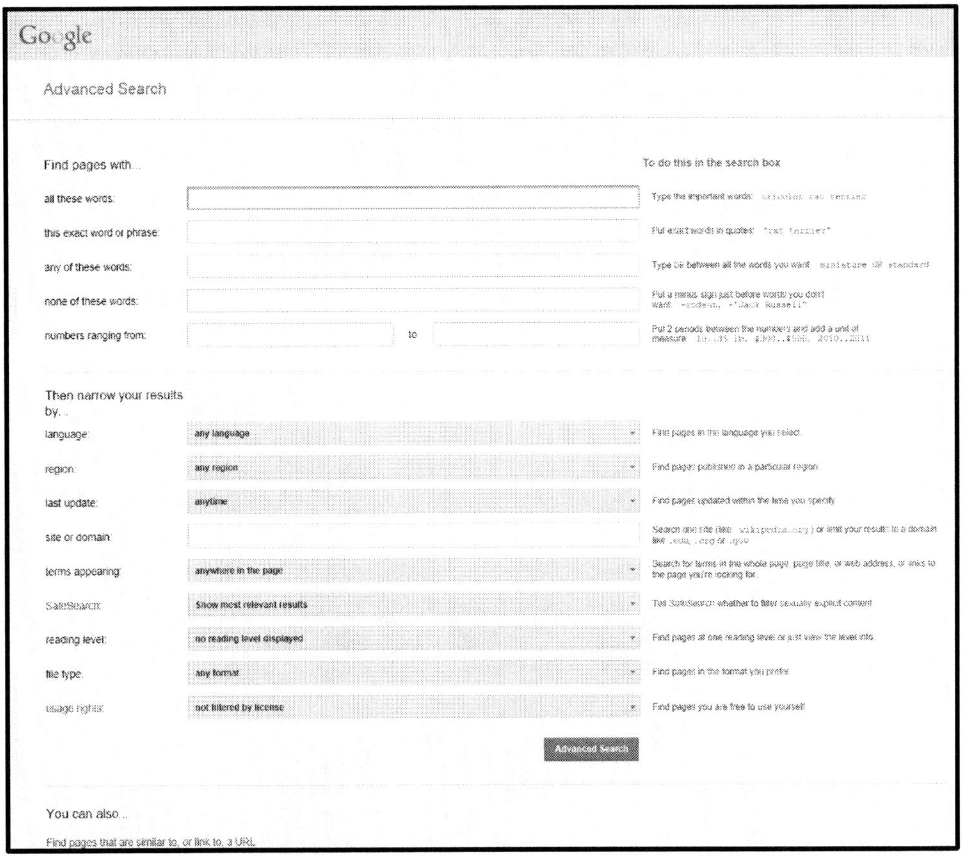

Figure 2-5

Google and the Google logo are registered trademarks of Google, Inc., used with permission.

Chapter 3

Case Law

Quick Start Page

Google Scholar is a good free resource for case law. You can search by topic, citation, or party names. You can narrow your jurisdiction before or after you search. You can even create alerts for your search. Just be sure to choose the Case Law button under the search box.

www.scholar.google.com

For more on finding cases free online, please read on...

Case Law

One of the biggest, and to many, most welcome additions to the body of free legal materials on the internet is case law. Previously only available on fee-based databases such as Westlaw or Lexis, most appellate court decisions are now available free on sources such as Google Scholar.

Breaking decisions are often posted online at court or other websites as soon as they are announced, sometimes becoming available on these free sources before the fee-based databases have them. In addition, some case decisions, such as trial level cases, may only be available on free sources.

Case Law 101: Before you start looking for cases, though, just a brief refresher on case law reporting:

Most cases that are reported in the print reporters that you find in a good law library – or in the pay databases – are appellate cases, cases that have already gone to court, been decided (in one way or another), and been appealed.

There are exceptions, however. The most obvious one is that you can find many trial level decisions from the federal district courts, which are reported in the Federal Supplement (F. Supp.) sets.

Other exceptions are administrative decisions and those from specialized courts such as tax and bankruptcy cases, which have their own print reporters.

For the most part, decisions of state *trial* courts are not usually reported. There are a few reasons for this, the main one being that there are just so darn many of them; also, most trial verdicts are announced from the bench, without a written determination set out in print. As with anything involving law, however – there are always exceptions! If the case involves an unsettled or developing area of law, the court may decide to issue a written decision. In print, these are often found only in state publications (e.g., Florida Law Weekly Supplement), and only a small number of cases are reported this way.

Other types of cases can also be hard to find, including:

Old cases, such as early British cases establishing the common law;

Cases from other countries;

Cases from international or foreign courts.

All of this shows why the promise of free case law on the internet is so wonderful. In one place, you can search for, read and update the cases that you may have had to visit a library to get, or pay to find on a commercial legal database. In addition, besides the usual reported appellate cases, the internet is your best bet for finding – again, free – old or foreign cases that a library might not have, brand-new cases that have just been announced, and even some trial level case decisions. Ready to start searching?

Google Scholar – www.scholar.google.com

At this time, Google Scholar may be your best bet for finding the type of cases the fee-based databases specialize in – appellate level from throughout the United States – but for free. It's extremely easy to search; the results can be easily categorized and sorted; you can even view your case citations in Bluebook format! To use Scholar, go to the site and *click on the button for case law*. Be sure that you choose the button for case law, as this is not the default setting. (see Figure 3-1) At this point, you may be offered the option to select the courts you want. You can also do this after first receiving your search results, if you'd rather wait to see what you get. Selecting the courts is simple, it is just a matter of checking the ones you specifically want your search to cover.

18

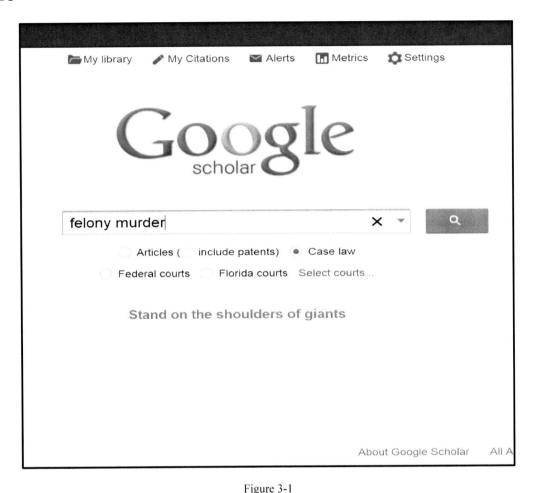

Figure 3-1

Google and the Google logo are registered trademarks of Google, Inc., used with permission.

Quick tip: Searching on Scholar is a bit more free-form than you might be used to. You can search by topic, case citation, or by party name. But you don't have a specific format to use, and can just type in the words you want to find. Here are a few handy tips:

- Use quotation marks around a phrase you want to find – e.g., "proximate cause" or "robinson-patman act".
- If looking for a case where you have a particular statute number, type in the number; allow some wiggle room (our Jello Rule) since a court might cite laws a bit differently than you expect. So, e.g., instead of typing: "42 U.S.C. §1395" try entering: 42 code 1395. You can easily browse your results from the search, and then narrow them down, or add to the search query and run it again.
- Always remember to look at the left-hand column of your search results screen! This is where you can restrict your results by jurisdiction or date.

As you look at the screen with your search results, you'll notice several things, including date and court restrictors, to your left. (see Figure 3-2) You'll also see, for each case in your list, the case information and some text from it.

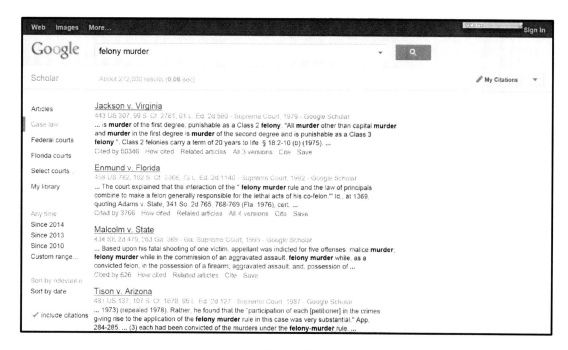

Figure 3-2

Google and the Google logo are registered trademarks of Google, Inc., used with permission.

And the cases themselves? Simply click on a case name from your results list to open it up. You'll get the entire case decision, minus any editorial enhancements you might get from the pay databases (so no headnotes or outline of the major points of the decision). (see Figure 3-3)

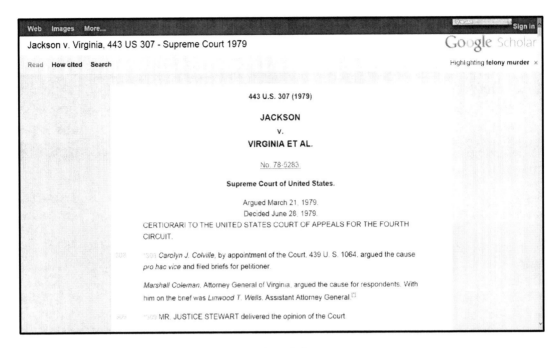

Figure 3-3

Google and the Google logo are registered trademarks of Google, Inc., used with permission.

You'll also find, for each case:

page numbering in the left margin that corresponds with that in the printed reporter, making it possible to do pinpoint cites to specific pages of the opinion;

hyperlinks to most authority cited within the case, so that you can quickly jump to a case, statute or other source used in the decision;

highlighting of your terms (which can be turned off if desired);

a 'how cited' link at the top left of the case, that will show you other cases where yours has been used, and how. (see Figure 3-4)

Regarding updating cases, while Google Scholar doesn't have a 'cite checker' per se, to check your cases and to see if they're still good law, we've both had great results from just using the How Cited link. Want another way to check your authority? Use the case name or case citation as your search term and put them in quotation marks, and look at those results; you can use the restrictions area on the left of the results screen to narrow your results by date, getting only the latest cases citing yours.

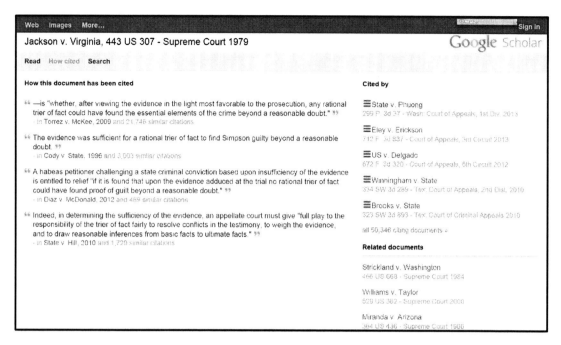

Figure 3-4

Google and the Google logo are registered trademarks of Google, Inc., used with permission.

Court Sites

While Google Scholar may be your answer for finding cases that have already made it into print, what if you're instead looking for other kinds of cases, such as those newly announced or even some that are at trial level and not ordinarily printed in the national reporters?

For those, you want to look at the individual court sites, whether for a mid-level state appellate court, a county court, even the United States Supreme Court. Appellate court web sites, for the most part, are updated frequently as new opinions are announced, and may be quicker at providing you with the opinions than fee-based databases are.

To locate a court's web site, you can try just typing the name of a court into a search engine. However, you might bring up several unrelated and irrelevant results, although the link to THE official court system will probably come up…eventually. (Also, you may not know the exact name of the court that you want….we know, it's happened to us too!)

To get a good listing of each state's official court sites, as well as information about each state's judicial system, try Cornell's Legal Information Institute (LII).

www.law.cornell.edu. Click on State Law Sources on the main page; once there, click on 'listings by jurisdiction' to get to the main sources for each state, including a link for the courts.

Another site for getting to the courts is American Law Sources Online. www.lawsource.com (see Figure 3-5)

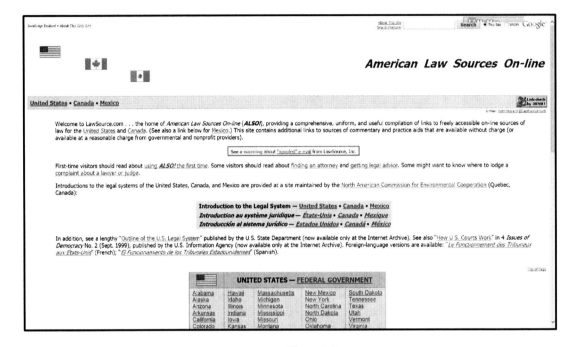

Figure 3-5

Law Source, Inc.

Each state page on the ALSO site contains links for its major legal and government sites, including information about each state's court system from the National Center for State Courts. www.ncsc.org

The links to state court systems will, for most states, take you to an official web site for the courts, similar to the one at www.flcourts.org.

Obviously, a court's web site is handy to look at for the information you might expect, such as names and biographical information of the judges, contact information for the court staff, some basic background about the kinds of cases the court deals with, and its schedule.

However, keep in mind that many courts issue their opinions online very soon after they're announced.

Look at the court's home page for a link such as 'opinions', 'recent decisions', or the like. Some courts issue the opinions online immediately, especially if the case is one of some importance. Some may put their opinions online on a regular basis, such as a set time each week. The web site should give you this information.

You may also find at a court's web site – particularly if it's a higher-level appellate court, such as a state supreme court – briefs that have been filed in the case, or other matters relating to the court opinions.

> **Quick Tip**: When looking at a judiciary web site, particularly one for a state court system, look for pull-down menus at the top or side of the page, listing the types of courts within that system. Going to the type of court – e.g., a listing for the family courts within a state – will help you more quickly find the court information, opinions, dockets, etc. that you may be looking for.

Finding trial level opinions

What about opinions from lower courts, such as trial level cases? You probably want to first try the actual court's web site (remember, you can look for the main page for the state judiciary, as shown above, and go from there); IF the case was an important one, or had been in the news, or dealt with an issue of first impression, there is a possibility that perhaps the court which heard the case put the decision on its web site.

Try the trial court's web site first. Even if the decision is not there (there may not have been an actual written opinion, after all), you still may be able to find out some other information that will lead you to the court information about the case. For example, many trial court systems have free online access to some court records, so that you could see who brought an action against whom, what the outcome was, date, costs, etc.

Sometimes, just a regular search engine, such as Google, may find what you need. Try a search using the name of the case, name of one or two parties, docket number, or some of the facts you're sure of and location. Use advanced search features if available for the search engine, to get the best results. E.g.: a Google search for *kantaras v kantaras filetype:pdf* brings up scanned documents in a notable Florida trial case, including the entire 817 page court decision. (The 'filetype:pdf' command is one that Google will attach to your search phrase when you use the advanced search features to specify that you only want pdf documents.) You can find out more about using advanced features in our section about effective searching.

Finding non-United States cases

Occasionally, you might find yourself faced with what seems to be an insurmountable challenge: you need to find case law from a court of another country. Whether looking for old English cases setting out common law principles, cases from an international tribunal, or cases from a particular foreign country, here are some things to try:

If looking for anything involving Canadian or Mexican law, start at ALSO www.lawsource.com, which truly is 'American', not just United States. It also has links for laws and cases of United States territories.

Remember the Cornell LII site mentioned a few sections ago in this chapter? It also has an area devoted to world law, at http://www.law.cornell.edu/world . On that page, the category 'National Law Material' allows you to pick out a particular area of the world and go to a list of countries and their legal resources.

Using a search engine to find cases

If you have some specifics about a particular case, you may want to try a regular internet search engine to look for the case. E.g., if you have a docket number, try typing that into a search engine such as Google. You can also try this with the name of a party or parties, or some of the facts of the case. Even if the case is not on Google Scholar, because of its age or the jurisdiction, this may give you a link to another site that has the case.

Using Wikipedia to find cases

Often when you're trying to find law, the easiest and quickest ways seem too obvious and are overlooked. But here's a trick you may not have thought of: if the case is even somewhat well-known, or if one of the parties to it is, look on Wikipedia! Go to www.Wikipedia.org ; use the search box on the home page – or on the top left, if already at an entry - and type in the name of the case, or parties, or even the legal principle you need to research. Now, there's no guarantee that you'll find what you need, but it's worth a try.

For example, let's say you're having fond memories of your first year Contracts class and want to reread the Carbolic Smoke Ball case. The case won't be on Google Scholar – it's a British case, and an old one to boot! So instead, try going onto Wikipedia and typing in

'Carbolic Smoke Ball'. Here's what you'll see: an entire page telling about the case, what the facts were, what the court's opinion stated, and what this led to in the development of the common law of contracts. You'll also get a direct link to the complete case opinion itself, as given on the web site of BAILII (British and Irish Legal Information Institute).

We'll be talking a bit more about Wikipedia in a later chapter, but the main things to remember about it are:

It can be a very quick way to find case or statute citations, and links to take you directly to those.

The explanations or analysis of those, however, may be incomplete, so don't depend on the text of the actual Wikipedia entry by itself; just as with headnotes or other editorial matter that has been added to help explain cases, the explanation someone else gives is no substitute for reading it yourself. Use Wikipedia, if possible, to find where the law is – but read and analyze it yourself.

Using Zimmerman's Research Guide to find case law

Zimmerman's Research Guide, at http://law.lexisnexis.com/infopro/zimmermans/ is a gold mine for legal researchers wanting ideas of where to look. (see Figure 3-6) Zimmerman's – which, though on the Lexis web site, is not biased towards Lexis nor any one type of legal source – provides an alphabetical list of contents, along with a search box to use if you aren't sure which category might have what you need. Among the other categories, which include a host of legal topics, the Guide has entries for different jurisdictions, including states and countries.

Figure 3-6

Zimmerman's Research Guide hosted by LexisNexis InfoPro

Zimmerman's can be a great starting place when trying to find cases on specific legal subjects. It specifies which free sites, if any, you can find the cases on, as well as any other places (pay databases, print materials, etc.) that will have the information you want. Often Zimmerman's also provides links to research guides on other web sites specific to your legal topic. For example, the Civilian Board of Contract Appeals website provides its own cases and Zimmerman's will give you a link to that site. (see Figure 3-7)

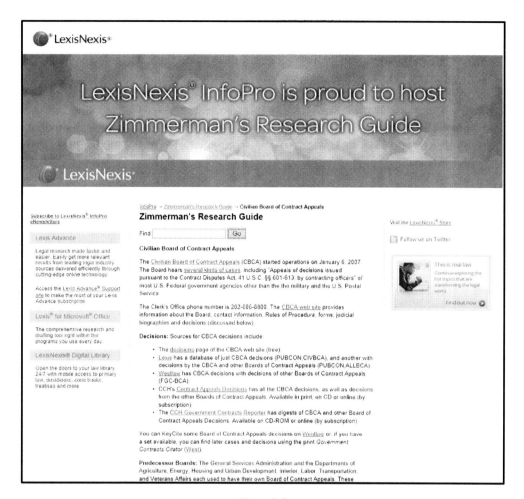

Figure 3-7

Zimmerman's Research Guide hosted by LexisNexis InfoPro

Quick tip: You may have already noticed, or will soon, that we refer to some sites several times, in different areas of this book. The fact is, some sites – particularly **ALSO!**, **Cornell's LII**, and **Zimmerman's Research Guide** – are excellent portals to other, more specific sites. Not only are they wonderful places to begin your research, but the names and URLs (at least with ALSO! and the Cornell site) are easy to remember, so that you don't have to fill your head or your favorites list with names and web sites. Just use these portals instead to get to the sites you need!

Some words about FastCase

Most state bar associations now include a subscription database, such as FastCase or CaseMaker, as part of their membership package. If you're used to using FastCase, but have access only to your state's cases with your subscription, you might want to check out the Public Library of Law. www.plol.org This site has free access to federal and state cases, court rules and statutes, and while the range of case law is more restricted by date than on other sites (e.g., some states only go back to 1997 or so), this can be quite handy, esp. for those already familiar with FastCase.

Court documents – finding them free on the internet

As noted before, a court's web site will sometimes contain documents that have been filed with that court, particularly appellate briefs for cases already decided. What if you want to see more than just a brief, though? What if the court doesn't include that paperwork on its page, or if the case is ongoing, or has been settled?

Using the advanced features on Google – or another search engine with 'format' specification features – you can often find court filings if they have been scanned onto the internet by a court or by a party to the case, or even an interested group that wants to make such pleadings available.

Most documents that are uploaded to the internet have been put on using Adobe's Portable Document Format, or pdf. By specifying that you want your search to only find results in pdf format, you're going to retrieve things that have been scanned onto the internet – things such as articles or files from print sources, including court documents and legal papers. Using Google's advanced search features, you can narrow your results to pdf and possibly bring up the filings in a particular case, or on a specific topic. To get to Google Advanced Search just go to www.google.com/advanced_search (see Figure 3-8) or after conducting a search look for the sprocket in the top right corner and from there select Advanced Search. (see Figure 3-9)

Google Advanced Search takes the place of Boolean searching where you used to have to construct long search strings with various connectors. Now you have different fields, clearly labeled. You just type into those fields, or choose from the pull down menus, exactly what you want. If you like doing the Boolean searching or want to learn how, to the right of the fields Google gives a description of how to type those connectors into the search box for yourself. But you can certainly just use the fields and Google will do the rest for you.

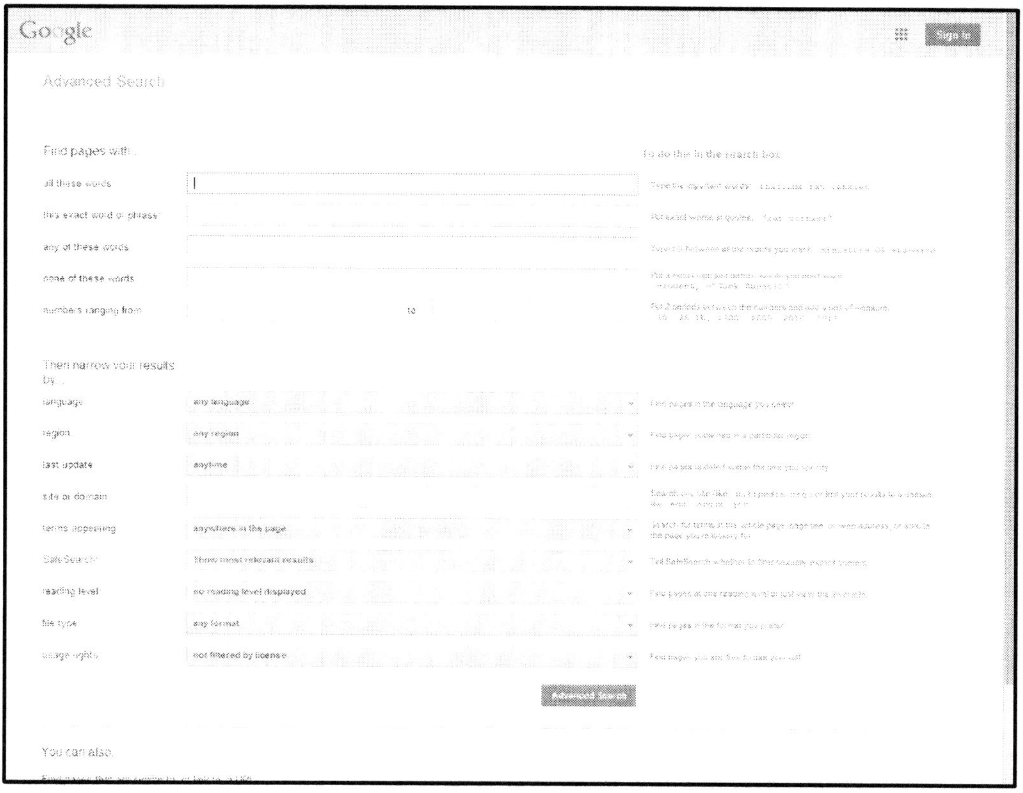

29

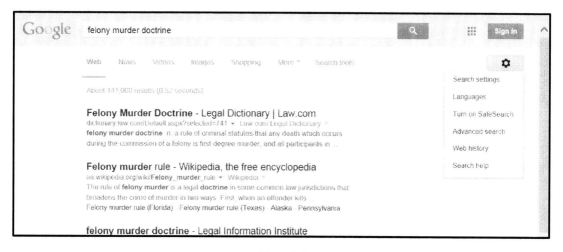

Figure 3-8

Google and the Google logo are registered trademarks of Google, Inc., used with permission.

Figure 3-9

Google and the Google logo are registered trademarks of Google, Inc., used with permission.

Chapter 4

Statutes

Quick Start Page

For federal statutes, a good place to start is the Government Printing Office's FDSys, or Federal Digital System. You can search the U.S. Code using quick search, advanced search, or search by citation features in the center of the page. You can also browse the code using the menu on the right side of the page.

www.fdsys.gov

For state statutes, you can start with American Law Sources Online (ALSO) at this link and then choose your state.

www.lawsource.com

You can also use your favorite search engine to search for "U.S. Code" or "your state here statutes".

To find out more about federal and state statutes, how they are made, and where to find them online for free, please read on…

Statutes

On the federal level we have a bicameral legislature (2 houses) of elected representatives. The House of Representatives has 435 members, elected every two years from the 50 states, according to each state's total population. The Senate has 100 members, two from each state regardless of the population. A senator's term of office is six years. Each senator and each representative has one vote. A Congress (a meeting of the federal legislature) lasts two years and begins the January after the election for members of the House of Representatives. So, if you ever wondered why they have those funny numbers for each Congress, that's why. We'll talk more about this when we look at citations for legislation. Each Congress is divided into two regular sessions. Anyone can propose or write a bill, but only members of the legislature can introduce them for consideration. Generally a bill may originate in the House or the Senate. The one exception is that bills for raising revenue must originate in the House.

A bill that originates in the House is designated by H.R. (for House of Representatives) then a number. A bill that originates in the Senate is designated by S. (for Senate) then a number. If you hear talk about a "companion bill", that is a bill with similar subject matter that is introduced into both houses at the same time. Why would they do this? It could be a matter of some urgency and the legislators want to hurry it along. Or, keep in mind this is a political process, it could be that multiple legislators want to have their own name on the bill and they are trying to beat each other to the punch. It's much the same when you listen to Congressional hearings and the legislators ask the same questions over and over again. It's not that they didn't hear the answer the first time. It's that each one wants to be on record as "asking the tough questions".

Let's get back to the process. A bill is introduced into one house or the other, assigned a number by the clerk, and then it is sent to committee. Depending on the subject matter of the bill, the special committees are the ones who gather information, hold hearings, draft amendments, and generally do all the hard work of legislating. Because of this, committee reports can hold a wealth of information for the researcher. Have you found the statute that rules in your case, but it doesn't really sound the way you need it to sound? Research the history of that statute. See if you can locate committee reports to find out the intent of the statute and the kind of language that was argued over. How did it read originally? What was added or removed? We will look at free online sources for committee reports.

Once the committee is done with a bill, it will report back to the floor favorably ("we think you should vote yes"), adversely ("we think you should vote no"), or without recommendation. All members of that house then vote on the bill and if it passes, it goes to the other house. So, if it starts in the Senate and passes, next it goes to the House of Representatives. If it starts in the House of Representatives, and it passes, the next stop is the Senate. Once it is agreed to in identical form by both the

House of Representatives and the Senate, it goes to the President of the United States. A bill becomes law when it is signed by the President. It may also become law if not returned to Congress by the President with objections within 10 days. If the President vetoes a bill (specifically rejects it with a "no"), the bill goes back to Congress. It can still be passed by an over-riding vote of the members of Congress. That requires a 2/3 vote in both houses.

Let us assume that it passed. This is where we, the researchers, enter the picture. What are we wading through in terms of Congressional documents? The very first time a new law is published, it is called a "slip law". That is a stand-alone version. The next time it is published is in something called "session laws". Those are all the laws passed, in chronological order, in a particular session of Congress. These are numbered starting with the number of Congress. For example: Pub. L. 112-1, Pub. L. 112-2, Pub. L. 112-3, etc. So, these public laws, abbreviated Pub. L., would be from the 112th Congress and would be the first, second, and third laws passed in that session. At this point the citations have nothing to do with the subject matter. These just signify when and in what order they were passed.

Session laws at the federal level are published in something (it used to be just a set of print books, now it's digital also) called the U.S. Statutes at Large. Those citations look something like this. 122 Stat. 3 That would be volume 122 of the U.S. Statutes at Large starting on page 3. So, the Pub. L. citation is *what* you are looking for, and the Stat. citation is *where* it lives.

The next place a law is published is in the United States Code. Finally! Something we all recognize! Once the session law is published as it was passed, in its entirety, then that law gets broken apart by subject matter and put into the existing U.S. Code. This is where we can search by topic. So, if the law contained some criminal law parts, and some procedural parts, and some tax parts, those would all go where they belong with similar topics in the Code. Each time you read a section of the U.S. Code it will refer you back to the Pub. L. number. That way if you need to read the whole thing as it was passed, so you can see how the parts relate to one another, you'll be able to do that. Code citations look like this: 26 U.S.C. §170.

So, for a quick review: a bill gets introduced, assigned a number, and goes to committee. The committee argues over it, reports back to the floor, and a vote is held. It passes and goes to the other house. Repeat. It passes both houses and goes to the President. The President signs it into law. It gets published as a slip law, then in the session laws for that session of Congress. Finally, it gets divided up and put into the existing U.S. Code according to topic. Whew.

A very similar process happens on the state level. Your own state's legislative website will likely have lots more particular details. One interesting thing to note here, is that we do have a state with a unicameral legislature (that is, it has only one house), and that state is Nebraska!

So, where to find all of these great things online? As always, start with the source if you can. Go right to the website of whatever legislative body produced the law that you are researching. A great place to start looking for statutes on the federal level is the Government Printing Office's Federal Digital System. www.fdsys.gov (see Figure 4-1) You will see this source throughout the book, as it is sort of a one-stop-shop for federal legal materials. It has search and browse functions, as well as advanced search, and search by citation features. The search by citation can really help keep you out of trouble. It will present you with a template. That way you don't have to worry about abbreviating incorrectly. Not that we ever do that (*all the time*).

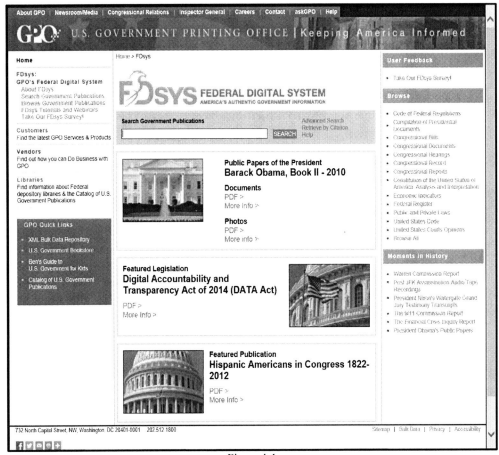

Figure 4-1
Federal Digital System from the U.S. Government Printing Office

If you are looking for the background information of a statute or are tracking a bill through the process, then www.congress.gov is where you should start. (see Figure 4-2) If you are familiar with the old Thomas website from the Library of Congress, this is the new zippy version! This is a great website with information about the members of Congress, committees, bills, laws that have been passed, the floor activities, roll call votes, and hearing schedules. You can find committee reports here.

You can even watch live streaming video of the happenings in Congress. This feature is great for any of you who have ever actually recorded the cable channel C-SPAN using your VHS recorder or your DVR. One of your authors is, in fact, just that nerdy. We won't tell you which one.

On the state level, the strategy is the same. Go right to the state legislature's website if you can. If you need help finding your state legislature's website, try www.lawsource.com and click on your state. (see Figure 4-3) Or do a quick search using your favorite search engine and type in something like "name of your state legislature". Then look through the results for something that says it is the official state legislature website. This is where the lawsource.com website really helps. It has already sorted out the official sources for you. An example of a state legislative website is Florida's Online Sunshine. http://www.leg.state.fl.us You will notice in the web address that you have legislature, state, Florida, and U.S., so it looks like an official government web address. Once you click on the link and get to the Online Sunshine webpage, you'll see search and browse options. There are links to the state House of Representatives and Senate websites. Also, most people come to this site looking for state statutes, so that search function is at the center on the top of the page. There is a pull down menu to choose the year. Notice that it only goes back to 1997. For most people that is plenty. If you need older statutes, check with a law library in your area. You may also notice, even state legislatures have live streaming video of legislative activities. If you come home in the afternoon to find your children online watching the state legislature, you should probably be deeply concerned.

Figure 4-2
Congress.gov

Just a brief note to wrap up this chapter, we have sort of glossed over the fact that there are constitutions on both the federal and state level. They do still exist! Normally you can find the constitution anywhere you also find statutes. If there is a great outcry from you, our trusty readers, at the lack of constitutional coverage… we will be sure to include it in the next edition of the book.

American Law Sources On-line

United States • Canada • Mexico

E-mail: Administrator@LawSource.com

Welcome to LawSource.com . . . the home of *American Law Sources On-line* (**ALSO!**), providing a comprehensive, uniform, and useful compilation of links to freely accessible on-line sources of law for the United States and Canada. (See also a link below for Mexico.) This site contains additional links to sources of commentary and practice aids that are available without charge (or available at a reasonable charge from governmental and nonprofit providers).

See a warning about "spoofed" e-mail from LawSource, Inc.

First-time visitors should read about using *ALSO!* the first time. Some visitors should read about finding an attorney and getting legal advice. Some might want to know where to lodge a complaint about a lawyer or judge.

Introductions to the legal systems of the United States, Canada, and Mexico are provided at a site maintained by the North American Commission for Environmental Cooperation (Quebec, Canada):

Introduction to the Legal System — United States • Canada • Mexico
Introduction au système juridique — États-Unis • Canada • Mexique
Introducción al sistema jurídico — Estados Unidos • Canadá • México

In addition, see a lengthy "Outline of the U.S. Legal System" published by the U.S. State Department (now available only at the Internet Archive). See also "How U.S. Courts Work" in 4 *Issues of Democracy* No. 2 (Sept. 1999), published by the U.S. Information Agency (now available only at the Internet Archive). Foreign-language versions are available: "*Le Fonctionnement des Tribunaux aux Etats-Unis*" (French); "*El Funcionamiento de los Tribunales Estadounidenses*" (Spanish).

Top of Page

UNITED STATES — FEDERAL GOVERNMENT

Alabama	Hawaii	Massachusetts	New Mexico	South Dakota
Alaska	Idaho	Michigan	New York	Tennessee
Arizona	Illinois	Minnesota	North Carolina	Texas
Arkansas	Indiana	Mississippi	North Dakota	Utah
California	Iowa	Missouri	Ohio	Vermont
Colorado	Kansas	Montana	Oklahoma	Virginia
Connecticut	Kentucky	Nebraska	Oregon	Washington
Delaware	Louisiana	Nevada	Pennsylvania	West Virginia
Florida	Maine	New Hampshire	Rhode Island	Wisconsin
Georgia	Maryland	New Jersey	South Carolina	Wyoming

American Samoa • District of Columbia • Guam • Northern Mariana Islands
Puerto Rico • Virgin Islands

Figure 4-3

Law Source, Inc.

Chapter 5

Administrative Law

Quick Start page

The Code of Federal Regulations (C.F.R.), the Federal Register (Fed. Reg. or F.R.), and an updating service called the eCFR are all available online for free from the Government Printing Office's FDSys. Use the search box in the center of the page (don't forget to try out the advanced search options) or browse using the links on the right.

http://www.gpo.gov/fdsys/

To find state administrative resources, search by state at the American Law Sources Online website.

http://lawsource.com/also/

Also, remember "go to the source". If you are looking for regulations or administrative decisions from a particular agency, try going right to the individual agency's website.

For more about administrative law and how to find it free online, please read on…

Administrative Law

Administrative law comes from administrative agencies which are under the executive branch of the government. Agencies can act like legislatures and like courts. They can promulgate binding regulations that govern activities within their jurisdiction. They can also decide disputes between parties (often the agency and someone who objects to a regulation) on a case-by-case basis. When researching administrative law, the first order of business is to determine which agency governs your situation and find out what you can about that agency. Agencies have power delegated to them by the legislature through what are called enabling statutes. Enabling statutes will tell you the purpose and limits of the agency. When conducting statutory research, if you come across an enabling statute, that is your clue that you need to then search for administrative regulations. A great place to find background information on an agency is the agency's website. The website should give you the history, purpose, functions, and current events for the agency. Very often they will also have their regulations, administrative decisions, and procedures as well. In some instances the agency website search functions will work great. If they don't, you can always use Google advanced search http://www.google.com/advanced_search and type in the web address of the agency in the Site or Domain: field... so that Google searches just the agency website for you. (see Figure 5-1)

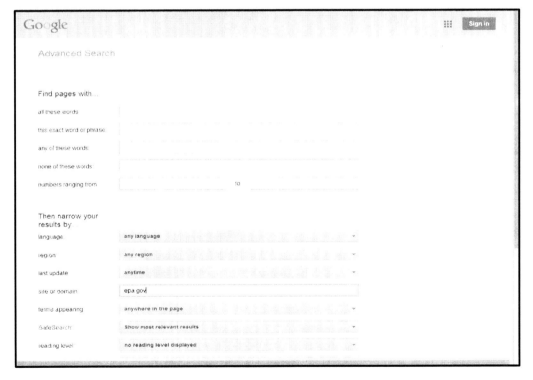

Figure 5-1

Google and the Google logo are registered trademarks of Google, Inc., used with permission.

A good way to find agency websites is to try their acronym and then put .gov on the end. For example the Environmental Protection Agency, or EPA, website is www.epa.gov . You can also do a search using the agency's name or acronym in your favorite search engine. For state agencies try a search like "Florida state agencies" then look through the search results for an official state page that gives you a list of the agencies and their contact information. The same can be done for federal agencies. A good directory of federal agencies can be found here. www.usa.gov USA.gov is the federal government's public portal and includes an A-Z list of federal agencies. An example of a state agency directory can be found here. http://www.myflorida.com/directory/ You may notice that this website ends in .com even though it is an official state website. The picture of the governor at the top of the page, along with the header The Official Portal of the State of Florida, will tell you that you have found a reliable source. To find more state administrative resources you can search by state at American Law Sources Online. www.lawsource.com (see Figure 5-2) You may also find which agency governs your situation when you see it mentioned in statutes, cases, or secondary information like practice guides or legal encyclopedia articles.

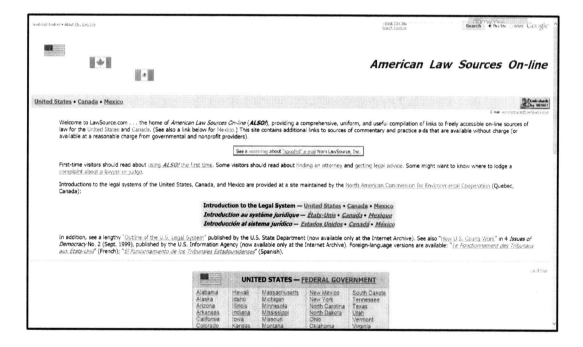

Figure 5-2

Law Source, Inc.

Let's talk some about the process. If you are interested in administrative law and how it all works, see the Administrative Procedure Act. http://www.archives.gov/federal-register/laws/administrative-procedure/

There are also state versions of this act. For example the Florida Administrative Procedure Act, Florida Statutes Chapter 120.
http://www.leg.state.fl.us/statutes/index.cfm?App_mode=Display_Statute&URL=0100-0199/0120/0120.html

Generally speaking, legislatures don't have the time and expertise to rule in every area. So, they delegate their authority to agencies that then gather the experts and conduct what is called notice-and-comment rulemaking. The agency will draft a proposed rule, then publish that rule and ask for comments. The draft may be amended multiple times. Once in its final form, the agency will publish the rule again with a notice that the rule will come into force on a particular date. All of these instances of publication happen in what is called a register. This is sort of a newspaper of all the "sausage making" that is administrative law. On the federal level this is called the Federal Register. Citations to the Federal Register will have the abbreviation Fed. Reg. or F.R. in them. Following our example for Florida, the newspaper of administrative workings was called Florida Administrative Weekly until October 2012, when it became a daily and changed its name to the Florida Administrative Register. So, for Florida you may see citations to F.A.W. (older than 2013) or F.A.R. (for newer entries).

Once the rule has been proposed, commented on, maybe amended, and finally approved to take effect… then it will be codified and placed into the Code of Federal Regulations by subject along with other similar topics. Those citations will abbreviate it C.F.R. On the Florida level the approved rule goes into the Florida Administrative Code, abbreviated F.A.C. This is where you would look for what is current binding administrative regulation.

When there are disputes over how the regulations are applied, and you know there will be disputes, there is usually an administrative process for hearings within an agency that must be exhausted before the parties can appeal outside the agency to the court system. To find these administrative decisions, you can look to specialty reporters, or the agency website itself.

To review, these are the places that you can expect to find administrative law materials: when conducting statutory research you may find enabling statutes that give rule-making authority to administrative agencies. In annotated statutes you may find reference to cases that interpret enabling statutes. In the Federal Register (Fed. Reg. or F.R.), or the state version of the administrative newspaper, you will find proposed rules and calls for comments. In the Code of Federal Regulations (C.F.R.) or the state equivalent, you will find regulations that are currently in force. Each regulation will have a history section that refers you back to the register, so that you can trace its creation through the notice-and-comment process. At the beginning of each CFR part, usually just below the table of contents, is an authority note showing the statutory authority under which the regulations have been issued. Following the authority note is a source note that provides the citation and the date of the Federal Register where the regulations were published. From that Federal Register section you may then trace the particular regulation back through the notice-and-comment process and find the preamble which gives background information and explanatory notes. Then for agency decisions when disputes arise, check the agency website, or a specialty reporter.

Administrative law really is a user friendly, highly participatory area of law. If you like political science and strategy, this may be an area for you!

Now that we know what we are looking for, let's talk about places to find it. The Government Printing Office's FDSys or Federal Digital System, is a great free resource right from the federal government. http://www.gpo.gov/fdsys/ (see Figure 5-3) You can search using the search box in the center of the page. Don't miss the Advanced Search option, and the Retrieve by Citation function. If you have a citation, for the C.F.R. or the Fed. Reg., you want to use Retrieve by Citation. If you want to browse, as you would through the books, so you can see all the sections in context, browsing is available from the menu on the right. Notice that there are the Code of Federal Regulations and the Federal Register.

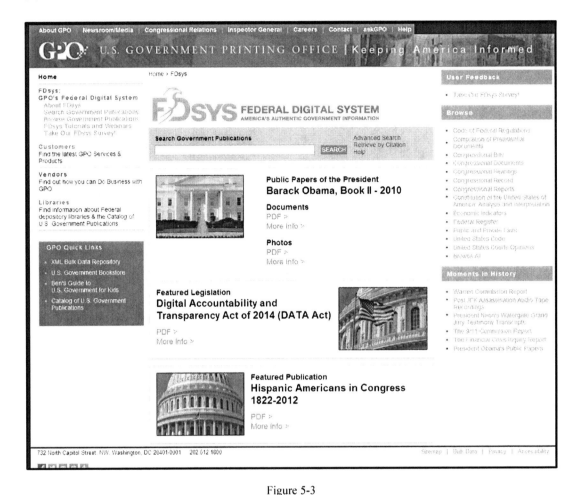

Figure 5-3

Federal Digital System from the U.S. Government Printing Office

For a free online way to be sure that your code sections are up to date, go to the Electronic Code of Federal Regulations (eCFR) website. http://www.ecfr.gov To participate in rule making by reviewing and submitting comments, go to http://www.regulations.gov As an example of state administrative resources, see Florida's regulations, administrative newspaper and administrative hearing decisions for free on www.flrules.org. You can browse or use the search boxes for both the Florida Administrative Code and the Florida Administrative Register, in the center of the page. Or you'll find a link to the Division of Administrative Hearings (DOAH) in the menu on the left hand side of the page. Here is that link. http://www.doah.state.fl.us/ALJ/ The DOAH is sort of an administrative decision clearinghouse for the state of Florida. Many of the Florida state agencies hold their hearing through the DOAH. It makes for a convenient central source to search. Once at the DOAH website you'll see a helpful menu on the left including a button for Case Search. One quick tip: on this particular website the default search has a box checked to Include Cases Dismissed Without Hearing. Unless you specifically want that, and you have nothing else to do with your weekend but to read through a gazillion cases, you may want to uncheck that box. The results will be much more manageable. You'll notice here there are lots of great ways to search, including by agency or by Administrative Law Judge (ALJ). This can be helpful if you have an upcoming hearing and want to get a feel for a particular agency or ALJ and how they do things. These kinds of search tips are something you'll want to discuss with your own law librarian. They'll know the best ways to search for legal information in your jurisdiction!

For administrative law sources in other states, try www.lawsource.com or do an internet search using your favorite search engine, i.e. "Google it", your-state-here state administrative law.

Chapter 6

Secondary Sources

Quick Start Page

American Law Sources Online (ALSO) is free and offers primary and secondary sources.

http://lawsource.com/also/

Cornell Legal Information Institute includes Wex, a free legal encyclopedia / dictionary.

http://www.law.cornell.edu/wex

Zimmerman's Research Guide, hosted by LexisNexis InfoPro, is a free legal research guide that will lead you to great sources by topic or jurisdiction.

http://law.lexisnexis.com/infopro/zimmermans/

For more about secondary sources, please keep reading…

Secondary Sources

A few definitions are probably in order. Secondary sources are not the law itself. They are commentary on the law, analysis of the law, and explanation of the law. They are also very helpful "go-withs" like forms and procedural guidance. If a legal topic is new to you, then you may want to start out with a secondary source. It should explain the area of the law to you, point out anything unusual, and then guide you to the best primary sources for that topic (the statutes, cases, and regulations that pertain). You will often hear the term treatise. This is not the same as treaties. A treatise is a book or set of books that discusses one topic in depth. Treaties are international legal agreements. So, when looking for secondary sources, a treatise on your chosen topic may be just what you need. There are many secondary sources that are not online for free, but that doesn't mean they are out of reach. This chapter is one of those instances when we will tell you about free online sources and we will also tell you about strategies for finding secondary sources that may be low cost online, or free to use in print.

Let's talk about the free online sources first. As you can tell by the Quick Start page for this chapter, there are a few websites that we feel are really good basic places to start. American Law Sources Online (ALSO) http://lawsource.com/also/ you will find mentioned throughout this book. (see Figure 6-1) It is a great aggregator of free online legal sources. Here you can find links to primary sources but also rules of procedure, codes of conduct, model jury instructions, explanation of court system structures, forms, and journals. It is arranged by U.S. federal government, the states, as well as Canada and Mexico.

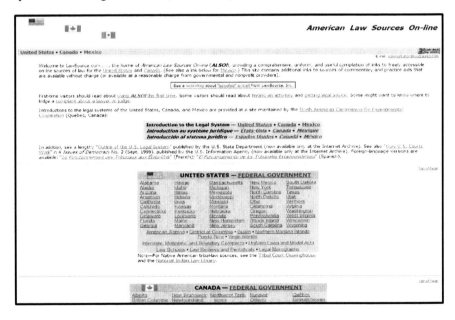

Figure 6-1

Law Source, Inc.

Cornell Legal Information Institute (LII) also provides both primary and secondary material. http://www.law.cornell.edu This website is part of the free access to law movement (FALM). http://www.falm.info/ You can read more about the movement at their website and see other websites that are part of the network. Cornell's LII has a free legal dictionary / encyclopedia called Wex, with options for both browsing and searching. http://www.law.cornell.edu/wex You may also decide that you like this concept so much that you want to participate, in which case there are options for editing and sponsoring content.

One of our other favorite starting places is Zimmerman's Research Guide. http://law.lexisnexis.com/infopro/zimmermans/ (see Figure 6-2) Even though this is hosted by LexisNexis, it is a free resource. Zimmerman's offers lots of legal research guides based on topic or jurisdiction. This is another source that you will see us talk about throughout the book. It gives you links to primary sources for your topic or jurisdiction. It will also give you the names of (and links to, if they're available) the leading secondary sources for your topic.

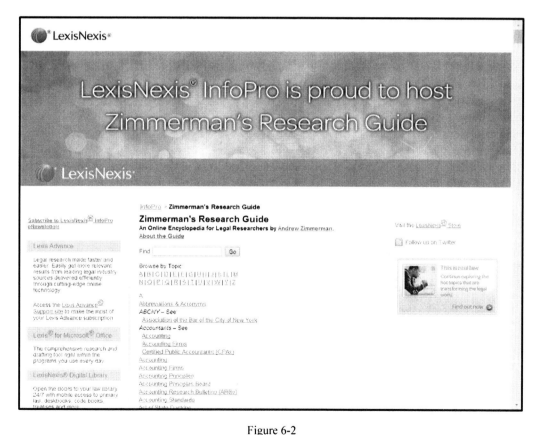

Figure 6-2

Zimmerman's Research Guide hosted by LexisNexis InfoPro

This is a good place to talk about "leading sources". If you have worked in a particular field for any length of time… or even from law school days… you may recognize certain leading treatises by the names of the authors. Some examples are "Nimmer on Copyright", "Couch on Insurance" or "Appleman on Insurance", "Moore's Federal Practice" or "Wright and Miller"; in Florida, "Trawick's Florida Practice and Procedure" and "Padovano's Florida Appellate Practice". These are the types of sources you'll find listed in the Zimmerman's Research Guides. He will tell you what the leading titles are. Finding them for free will be a challenge. If you are practicing in a particular area, you may consider buying one of these treatises for yourself. Owning your own may be more cost effective, if it is something that you will use frequently. That being said, you certainly want to test drive materials before you buy them. Don't forget about your friendly local law library. Law libraries are a great place to use these materials for free and become familiar with the ones that are most useful for your practice.

If you're not sure how to find a law library in your area, or one that has the treatise you need, now is a good time for us to talk about Worldcat. http://www.worldcat.org/ Most libraries now have gone digital. Even though we still have print books on the shelves, we have many electronic materials, too. Our library catalogs are also electronic. Gone are the days of the old wooden card catalogs… some of us still miss them. It's purely nostalgia. Those of us who were around long ago and had to file all of those little cards, in all of those little drawers, will quickly tell you that electronic catalogs are much better. Anyway, libraries that have electronic catalogs can now easily share that information with the world. One way is through Worldcat, which is literally a worldwide library catalog. It is free to use for anyone who has access to the internet. You will notice that you can set up a free account if you would like to set your preferences, keep track of searches, etc. However, it is not necessary to have an account in order to search. Worldcat will use your IP address in combination with your search terms, to tell you the closest library or libraries to your geographic location that have the material you need. You can reset the location by entering a postal code or city and rerunning the search. So, if you need a particular book today, you can find which library has it that is closest to you today. If you need the same book, but next week when you will be in a different city, enter the city and rerun the search. The search results will generally give you a link to the library's webpage as well, where you can find out more about their lending policies, if they are open to the public, if you can make photocopies and the like. The actual search result will tell you the distance each library is from your location, beginning with the closest, and will have links to map the location. This can be a great way to find law libraries in your city. Just run a search for something that you know will likely only be in a law library, and that is the type of library that you will find in the search results. For example, if you wanted to find the nearest public library you could run a search for Harry Potter. On the other hand, if you specifically wanted a law library you may want to search for Nimmer On Copyright or Moore's Federal Practice. These would likely give you a list of law libraries, and not public libraries. If public libraries are included in the list, the word Public is usually in the name, so you can differentiate.

In other chapters you will see that we recommend going right to the source of the legal information that you need. If you need statutes, go to the website for the legislature responsible for those statutes. If you need court opinions, try the court's website. If you need administrative regulations, try the agency website. The same is true for lots of great secondary sources. The people who are responsible for laws in a particular area are likely to have all of the explanatory material for those laws as well as great information on procedure, theory, challenges, and maybe even the preferred forms. Think about what entity deals with the law in question most often and go there first for helpful secondary information.

Legislatures

Legislature websites can be a great source of secondary information about the legislative process, bills that are being considered, and those that have passed (or not). Legislative websites often offer information about the legislators, contact information for their offices, committee pages with information about the work of the committees, committee members, and documents such as bill analysis. Many even offer streaming video of the legislative sessions in progress. If you need background information on legislation, as we have said many times throughout the book, go right to the source. You will be amazed at the wealth of material available to you. Using our Florida example, the state legislative website for Florida is called Online Sunshine. http://www.leg.state.fl.us For links to other states, try American Law Sources Online (ALSO) http://lawsource.com/also/ and search for your state. For United States federal legislative information, including members' profiles and contact information, the Congressional Record, and committee reports, try Congress.gov. (see Figure 6-3) http://beta.congress.gov/ The United States House of Representatives is here http://www.house.gov/ and the United States Senate is here https://www.senate.gov/ . But we recommend starting with Congress.gov as a great one-stop-shop for federal legislative information. For any of these websites, don't forget to check out the advanced search options.

Figure 6-3

Congress.gov

Courts

Speaking of court websites, obviously search for a website of any particular court where you will be practicing. That is where you will find rules of court, practical who-what-where information, and probably forms. Why pay for generic forms from a big national commercial database, when you may be able to get jurisdiction specific ones right from the court for free? As an example, we direct you to the Florida State Courts website. http://www.flcourts.org/ This site includes great information like a court locator where you can search by city or zip code, look at a list of locations or view them on a map. There are separate tabs for self-represented litigants, the court community, and the media. We don't have to tell you that all of these contain useful resources for attorneys. Just because something says it is for the public, doesn't mean attorneys can't use it too! The website also includes things like jurisdiction charts, court interpreter services, research and reference links, education and outreach, jury management, alternative dispute resolution, publications and statistics. For more, or to find your state courts website, try also the National Center for State Courts. http://www.ncsc.org/

For similar information on the federal level, try the United States Courts website. http://www.uscourts.gov It includes a court locator where you can search by city, state, zip code, or browse the map. There are tabs about rules and policies, judges and judgeships, statistics, forms and fees, court records, and educational resources. The forms are searchable by form number and category (civil, criminal, etc.) and the forms are fillable online. There is nothing so great as getting the appropriate form right from the court website. That way you know you have the preferred one! The U.S. Courts website also has a link to PACER (Public Access to Court Electronic Records) for filing electronically. Sadly, this is not free. But it is very low cost for retrieving court documents including filings, and if you're practicing in federal court you likely already have a PACER account for your own electronic filing.

Another great court website is the Federal Judicial Center which is the education and research agency for the federal courts. http://www.fjc.gov/ This website offers resources on federal judicial history as well as educational programs and materials. You may also want to check out the website for the United States Sentencing Commission. http://www.ussc.gov/

Agencies

Agency websites are not just a good source of agency specific regulations, but also all of the information that goes with those regulations… like procedures, forms, compliance reports, statistics, history… you name it. There is no one better to turn to for help in a particular area than those who deal with it every day. The same is true on both the federal and the state level. If you aren't sure which agency governs a particular area, try a simple web search for "federal agency directory" or "name of your state agency directory". This should get you an official source of the agencies and links to the individual agency websites. There are official sources for the administrative codes in their entirety (state and federal) that include all agencies. We talk more about those in the chapter on administrative law. But don't overlook the agencies themselves as they are excellent sources of the agency specific codes and so much more in the form of secondary sources! As an example the Florida Department of Environmental Protection is here. http://www.dep.state.fl.us/ The site offers a search function as well as a browsable index. There are tabs for citizens, educators, businesses, government, as well as the latest news and public notices. The United States Environmental Protection Agency website is very much the same. http://www.epa.gov/ You can conduct a specific search or browse by issue, learn about science and technology, access the laws and regulations, and participate in the administrative lawmaking process. One other tip, and this applies to any website that you visit, be sure to scroll down to the bottom of the page. There is usually a section at the very bottom with lots more great links!

Professional organizations

Professional organizations can be a great source of secondary information. Just think about who normally deals with the topic that you are researching. Then go to those people to see if they have information to share. Obviously, your state bar association is one good source. We will use the Florida Bar Association website as an example. https://www.floridabar.org/ (see Figure 6-4)

Figure 6-4

The Florida Bar

The Florida Bar website offers a lawyer directory. Tip for all of you practicing attorneys: fill out your online profile with the bar association. Not only is your online profile a great way for people to contact you, the more information you put in your profile, including a photo, if possible, the less likely that your professional identity will be stolen. You definitely don't want someone scamming "your" clients while pretending to be you, and having those poor folks think that you are the bad guy! The Florida Bar website also includes lots of great practice resources including LOMAS, the Law Office Management Assistance Service, as well as a CLE section where you can register for and report your CLE activities, tech tips, and the Florida Bar News and Florida Bar Journal. All of this is available online right from the bar association. It also has great sections for the public and for paralegals. Hint: attorneys can use these sections too!

The American Bar Association is another website worth visiting. http://www.americanbar.org Within the bar associations, look for specialty practice groups. They can offer a wealth of resources also. One more thing to remember... blogs. Blogs can be a great way to hear people who work in a particular field talk about the ins and outs of what is happening. Bar associations can be a great way to find legal specific blogs. Beyond bar associations, think of who else might deal with legal specific topics. One example would be for intellectual property, you might want to visit the United States Patent and Trademark Office website http://www.uspto.gov/ , the United States Copyright Office http://copyright.gov/ , or the World Intellectual Property Organization http://www.wipo.int .

Specialty libraries

There can also be specialty libraries out there ready and waiting to help you. If you aren't sure, ask your local librarian to help you find them. A couple of libraries come to mind. The United States Library of Congress is a fabulous resource available for free to anyone who has internet access. http://www.loc.gov Especially helpful is their Guide to Law Online. http://www.loc.gov/law/help/guide.php (see Figure 6-5)

Some others that might fall into this category of specialty libraries are the Homeland Security Digital Library https://www.hsdl.org which is just like it sounds. Or perhaps you would like to try the National Library of Medicine from the National Institutes of Health. https://www.nlm.nih.gov/ These are just a few limited examples. The resources are out there.

Figure 6-5

Library of Congress Guide to Law Online

Tips and strategies

Now let's put in a few extra tips for finding secondary sources. One really great way to get started researching a new area of the law is to do a Google search (or use your favorite search engine) and use the search terms "your topic legal research guide". Then be a wise consumer and sort through the results for reliable sources. If you aren't sure how to determine which ones are good, see the chapter on evaluating resources or ask your local librarian to help you. One favorite source of ours is reports by a group called the Congressional Research Service (CRS). These good folks do, just like it sounds, research for Congress. They don't make these reports for us… but the reports can be really helpful. Try doing a search for "your topic CRS report". If you find one, copy the title and run that as a search also. Very often the CRS will have done multiple versions of the same report, updating it through the years. If you don't have much luck searching for CRS reports outright, you may want to try a website that collects them. https://opencrs.com/

We may get hate mail over this next tip, but we actually find Wikipedia to be very helpful. https://www.wikipedia.org/ People will complain that the sources aren't reliable… but you need to evaluate every source that you use. We find that Wikipedia can give you a great introduction to a topic. Just check out their references for yourself (as you should with every source of information that you use). We are often guilty of scrolling to the bottom of a Wikipedia article first to check the links that are provided, before we read the article itself. And for those of you who are fascinated by collaborative information of this type, there is a project going on at Northwestern University that compares the content across Wikipedia articles from different countries and different languages. http://omnipedia.northwestern.edu/

Please don't forget about Google and all its specialty tools. Google Books is a good way to look inside, especially older, law books. http://books.google.com/ You can even search Google Books by topic, without a specific book title. (see Figure 6-6)

Figure 6-6

Google and the Google logo are registered trademarks of Google, Inc., used with permission.

There is also Google News which is a great way to find background information on a legal subject. http://news.google.com/ One more Google tip is to use Advanced Search http://www.google.com/advanced_search and narrow your file type to .pdf. Very often articles or even legal documents themselves are uploaded in .pdf. By searching for your topic and limiting the results to .pdf only, you can more easily wade through what might otherwise be thousands of results. (see Figure 6-7)

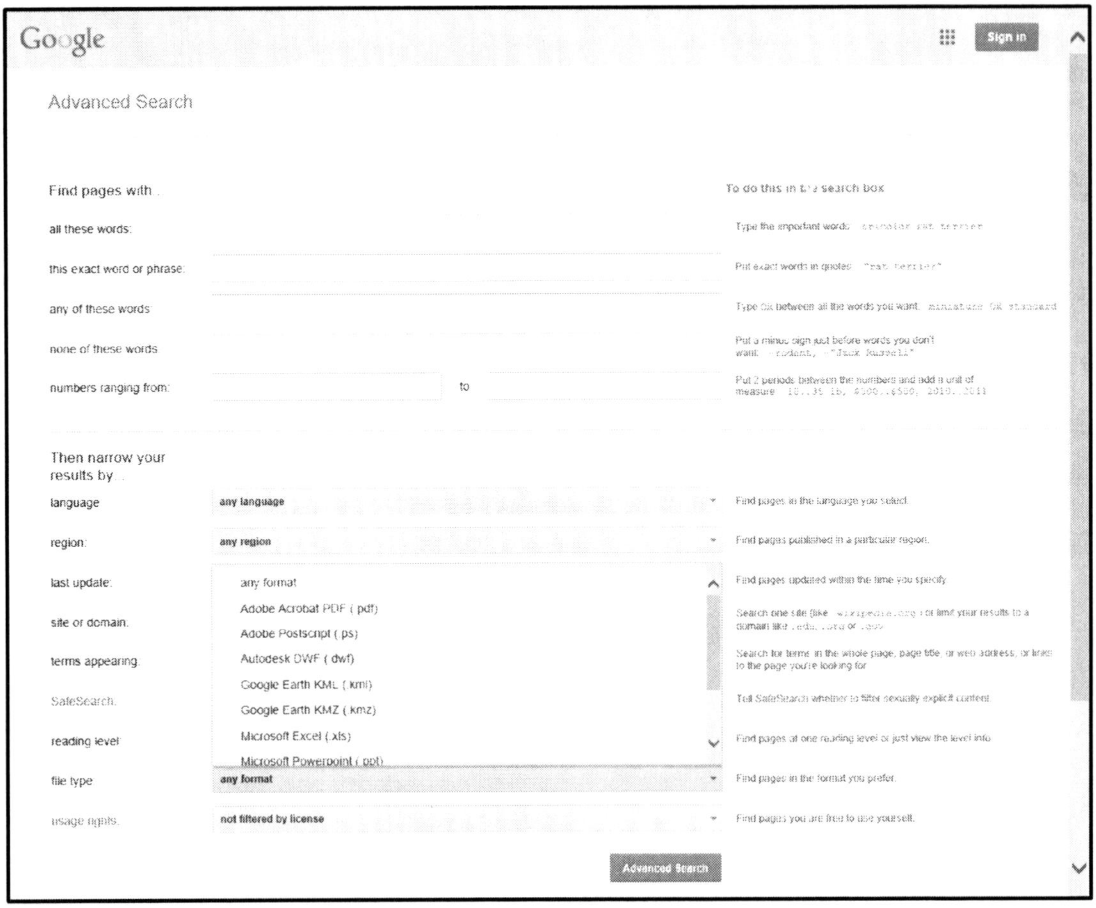

Figure 6-7

Google and the Google logo are registered trademarks of Google, Inc., used with permission.

There are just a couple of more tips. OK not really, we have hundreds. We talk about the Internet Archive throughout the book. https://archive.org It is an absolutely fascinating place to explore. Sometime ask us about Wanita's elderly one-handed Ukrainian neighbor who swims laps with her in the pool and wanted classical Russian music to load on his waterproof MP3 player… that's a whole other story. (Note: we found the music on the Internet Archive.) One of our favorite features of the Internet Archive is the Wayback Machine. You can enter a web address and then choose a date on the calendar to see how that website looked in the past. One great way to use the Wayba: very often journals will have their current issue on their website for free. Once the newest issue comes out, the older issue is moved to the "archive" and you have to pay for access. Use the Wayback Machine to go to the journal's website as it looked on the date of the article, and see if you can access it free that way. Time travel right from your computer! You can also use the Wayback Machine to access government webpages as they were in the past. Was there a great manual on an agency website and now it's not there? Go look at the webpage from a previous date. Government offices shut down due to sequestration or weather (grrr)? Use the Wayback Machine to visit the website from last week or last month.

OK, really just one more tip. We have talked about American Law Sources Online (ALSO) throughout the book. http://lawsource.com/also/ They give you access to secondary materials too. Look for the links that say Law Review and Periodicals or Legal Monographs.

Chapter 7

Foreign Law

Quick Start Page

The Library of Congress Guide to Law Online nations page – the United States Library of Congress Guide to Law Online has a wealth of information, including a page for finding legal materials from different nations.

http://www.loc.gov/law/help/guide/nations.php

New York University's GlobaLex has legal research guides for various nations.

http://www.nyulawglobal.org/globalex/#

For more on these topics, please read on...

Foreign Law

Let's start with a definition. Very frequently the question is posed, "What is the difference between foreign law and international law?" Foreign law is simply the domestic law of a country where you are not. So, if you are in the United States, then Mexican law is foreign law. On the other hand, if you are in Mexico, then U.S. law is foreign law. Foreign law sets out the parameters of the relationship between a country's government and its citizens. In that respect it can be thought of as vertical law. Generally, it is confined to the political boundaries of that one country. International law, by contrast, is the law that governs the relationship between sovereign nations. It can be thought of as horizontal law. If you are interested more in international law, please see that chapter. There are lots of great free online resources for both foreign and international law, and they understandably overlap quite a bit.

If we step back to our chapter on evaluating resources, you will see that we need to start with a plan. In researching foreign law, the first part of that research plan is to find out what type of legal system exists in your jurisdiction. There are several legal traditions or types of legal systems. The main two are civil law and common law. Generally, the United Kingdom and other nations that have been historically connected with it are common law jurisdictions. Most other nations are civil law jurisdictions. This, of course, is a vast oversimplification. For purposes of this book we will play sort of fast and loose with the definitions of the types of legal systems. In addition to these two main types of systems there are also religious law, customary law, and mixed legal systems. Mixed legal systems are just like they sound, where one or more of the other types may be found, sometimes overlapping, in the same geographic or political place. For example, the United States began as a common law jurisdiction. We have developed more and more sophisticated statutes, both state and federal. Also, the state of Louisiana is a civil law jurisdiction within the United States. So, technically speaking the U.S. has a mixed legal system. It turns out that humans, and the ways by which we relate to each other, can be quite complex. Who knew?

Please understand that the concept of legal systems is much more involved than we have portrayed and many people have made careers studying and debating the difference between systems. If you are intrigued and would like to know more, there are many great books available. In keeping with the free-online-resource theme of this book, you may want to visit Juriglobe from the University of Ottawa. http://www.juriglobe.ca/ (see Figure 7-1)

If you are a visual learner, as some of us are, you will appreciate Juriglobe's color coded world map of legal systems. The website itself is accessible in many languages. Besides the map, the website offers sections on legal systems classification, geographic distribution, United Nations member states legal systems, demographic distribution, world GDP and GNI per capita distribution, international trade and legal integration, languages and legal systems, as well as international linguistic spaces.

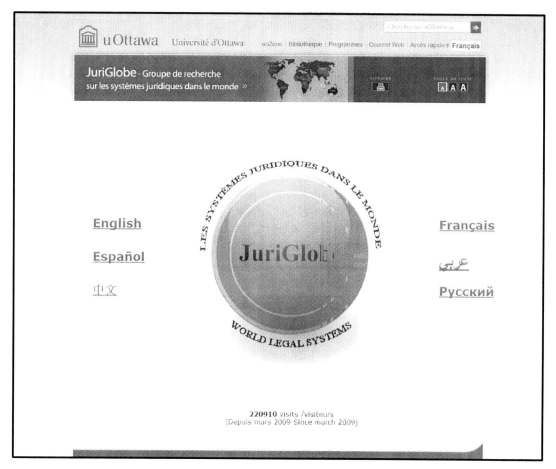

Figure 7-1

Univ. of Ottawa, Faculty of Law, Civil Law Section www.juriglobe.ca

Now, back to our task, to decide what type of legal system we are dealing with so that we'll know what type of documents to research. Very generally speaking, civil law jurisdictions have a comprehensive code and case law that is not binding on anyone except the parties to that case (no precedential value). So in civil law jurisdictions, you're looking for the code. In common law jurisdictions, you have some statutes but also case law that is binding on lower courts within the same jurisdiction. So, in common law systems you are looking for code and court opinions. Be sure to remember that there may be administrative regulations, local and federal, on top of that. For a more in depth understanding of what are legally binding materials within a particular country, you will want to look for a legal research guide specifically for that country.

64

To accomplish this type of research for free online we suggest starting with one of two main sources, though we will discuss many others that are also helpful. A good place to start is either the Library of Congress Guide to Law Online nations page http://www.loc.gov/law/help/guide/nations.php (see Figure 7-2) or New York University's GlobaLex http://www.nyulawglobal.org/globalex/# . The Library of Congress nations page has an alphabetical list of nations. When you click on a nation, the research guide will give you the names of (and links to, if available) the branches of government, official sources of law, and more in-depth research guides for that jurisdiction. If authoritative translations are available online, there will also be links for those. Translation issues are a subject that we will address in detail later in this chapter. The Library of Congress has many subject specialist librarians that can be a tremendous source of knowledge for you. If you don't immediately see what you need, contact them via the website! Real people work at these places and they have made careers helping researchers find what they need. Think of them as your favorite local librarians, who have gone virtual. Similarly, GlobaLex's foreign law page has an alphabetical list of nations with instructions on how to find legal resources for each. These are both good reliable quick-start ways to wade into foreign law research.

Figure 7-2

Library of Congress Guide to Law Online

Some more great sources are the World Legal Information Institute www.worldlii.org, the European Union's Eurlex http://new.eur-lex.europa.eu/homepage.html (more on this in the chapter on international law), and N-Lex (for specific European Union member countries' domestic laws) http://new.eur-lex.europa.eu/collection/n-law.html. The World Legal Information Institute is part of the Free Access to Law Movement http://www.fatlm.org/ , which is a group of organizations that provide and support free access to legal information around the globe. Many of these organizations, but not all, use the term Legal Information Institute or LII in their names. At either the World LII website or the FALM website you can find links to other websites in the collective. World LII offers access to legislation, case law, and treaties from around the world with many different methods of searching.

EurLex gives access to European Union law. The European Union (E.U.) is a supranational entity that is somewhat unique in the world, at least for now. The members give up some sovereignty in order to join, and there are varying degrees then of governing by the E.U. over the member states. In this context, the term "states" means sovereign nation states. Because the E.U. government is not meant to replace existing national governments, this is not precisely domestic law. Neither is it international law exactly, as the members have surrendered some sovereignty and agreed to be bound by E.U. law when they joined. So, for lack of being able to decide the appropriate category, we will discuss the European Union more in the chapter on international law... though it would just as easily fit here.

N-Lex is actually a database of purely domestic law of the member states of the E.U., so it is listed here. When you navigate to N-Lex, you will find a menu of the names of the member states. As you hover over each name a listing of the database contents will appear. You will notice that this is mostly legislation and will probably be only in the official language(s) of the state in question. Keep in mind the discussion we have had about legal traditions and that most countries will be concerned primarily with legislation rather than court opinions. Also, most countries write their legislation in their own language only, as it is meant for domestic use. We will talk more later about translations.

A few more sources and research tips are in order here. One resource that you will notice throughout this book is Zimmerman's Research Guide. http://law.lexisnexis.com/infopro/zimmermans/ (see Figure 7-3) Though Zimmerman's is hosted by LexisNexis, it is free. Many of the country guides will send you out to resources we have already discussed such as World LII and GlobaLex. Nevertheless, Zimmerman's is a great place to start, not only for foreign legal research, but subject matter legal research too. The thing we really like about Zimmerman's is that it gives you leads on the best sources, "the" titles in a particular area.

Another tip is to think of the subject matter of the law that you need. Is it about every day interactions between citizens, like family law, business, or taxes? Now think of who is likely to use that law and may have it available for you to view. A good place to look is the Department of State for the United States http://www.state.gov/, or the corresponding diplomatic arm of the government that you are researching. Very often these offices will have laws available that deal with areas of frequent interaction between citizens of their country and others. For example, the U.S. State Department has a legal considerations page. http://travel.state.gov/content/travel/english/legal-considerations.html

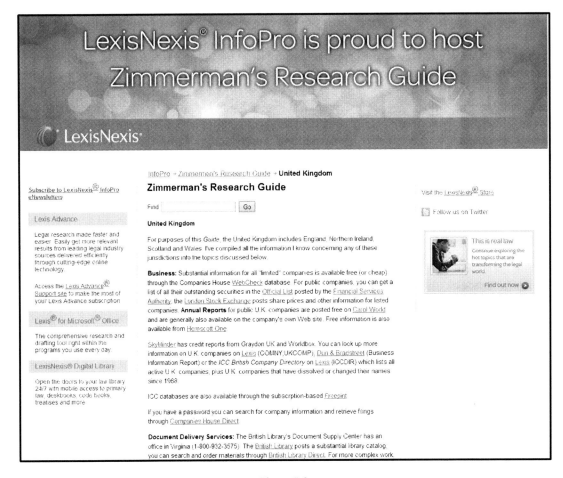

Figure 7-3

Zimmerman's Research Guide hosted by LexisNexis InfoPro

Think more about the subject matter of your legal research in the foreign jurisdiction. If you are looking for intellectual property law from another country, you may want to try the World Intellectual Property Organization (WIPO) http://www.wipo.int/portal/en/index.html

and their legal database WIPOLex. http://www.wipo.int/wipolex/en/ WIPOLex has both domestic intellectual property legislation from many countries, and treaties dealing with intellectual property agreements between nations. Similarly, if you were looking for labor and employment type laws from other countries, you may want to try the International Labour Organization (ILO) http://www.ilo.org/global/lang--en/index.htm and their database Natlex. http://www.ilo.org/dyn/natlex/natlex_browse.home Looking for food and agriculture laws? Try the Food and Agriculture Organization http://www.fao.org/home/en/ and their FAOLex. http://faolex.fao.org/faolex/ What about criminal law? Try the United Nations Office on Drugs and Crime (UNODC) https://www.unodc.org/unodc/index.html and their legal library's countries pages https://www.unodc.org/enl/browse_countries.jsp Don't forget about the World Legal Information Institute and that there are many country specific legal information institutes that you can link to from there (just scroll to the bottom of their page and click on the logos). http://worldlii.org/ Wanita's brother calls this the "NASCAR slide" because the logos look like the sponsor decals on the sides of race cars.

These are just a few examples. Many other resources exist. Think about your legal topic and the area of the world. You may find the information you need through either of those starting places… a subject guide, or a country guide. You will notice as you begin visiting these sites that many people are interested in making laws freely available to their constituents, whether those constituents are others in their same professional field, others who have similar advocacy interests, or simply citizens of their own country. You will also notice that these resources have multiple ways to access the information that they make available. Look for browse, search, and advanced search options.

One last tip before we talk about translations. If you haven't yet heard of it, you want to explore the Internet Archive https://archive.org/ and particularly the Wayback Machine. The Internet Archive is exactly like it sounds. They have an unbelievable archive of video, text, and audio files from the internet. The thing we want to tell you about here, though, is the Wayback Machine. For those of you old enough to remember (like us), the reference is to the cartoon of Mr. Peabody and Sherman. Mr. Peabody had a time travel device that he called the Wayback Machine. We know there is a more recent movie of the same story, but we are still nostalgic for the original cartoon and those carefree days of childhood. OK, back to work. The Internet Archive Wayback Machine has a search field where you can enter a web address and go back to see snapshots of that particular website as it looked on specific days in the past. When conducting foreign legal research, this can be helpful to see previous versions of government websites from the jurisdiction you are researching. We have also used it when the U.S. federal government offices have been shut down for one reason or another. Simply type in the address and look at the website as it was last week or last month. A fun experiment with the Wayback Machine is to search for previous versions of your favorite news website, or maybe your alma mater's website. We dare you not to spend the rest of today playing with this great website!

Finally we get to talk about translations. Obviously people write their own laws in their own language. We lawyers, being how we are, like to fight about the meaning of words. We like very detailed negotiated definitions for words. So when it comes to reading and using legal documents in a language other than our first, just any old translation won't do. We need authoritative, legally specific translations. The people who do the translating need to be fluent in both languages, also to have legal knowledge in both languages, and maybe have knowledge of multiple legal systems or traditions as well. As complex as legal drafting can be, imagine how much more so it becomes as you add multiple languages to the mix. What kind of translation you look for can depend on where you are in the process. There are machine translators that can help you decipher if you have the right document, but are not sufficient then for the legal work you must base on that document. For example, you are looking through a document that is not in your first language. You need to know if it is forestry regulations or a constitutional freedom of religion clause. You have no idea. A machine translator can help! Now that you know you have the right document and you get the gist of what it says, you need something much more authoritative before you quote sections of the document to build your legal argument. This is where you need to use some research strategies.

For the beginning searches, a couple of machine translators are readily available. Google Translate is pretty user friendly. http://translate.google.com/ As of this writing, it will translate to and from about eighty languages. There is a box into which you can type the words that you want to translate. You may also copy and paste words into the box. Google Translate will auto-detect the beginning language, which is very helpful if you have no idea what language it is. Don't laugh. This often happens. We call it the heck-if-I-know syndrome. You may also specifically choose the "from" language. Then for the second box you choose the "to" language and Google translates... loosely. So beware. Take the translation in the spirit in which it is offered. This is another website that is fun to play with... if you ever come back from playing with the Internet Archive. Try translating a paragraph, then translate it back and see if it still makes sense. Besides being fun, this will give you a sense of the limitations of Google Translate and help you to use it appropriately. Also, if you download the Google toolbar for your browser, or use Google Chrome as your browser, it will translate foreign webpages for you. Again, loosely.

Another machine translator, that many people don't realize they already have, is built into Microsoft Word. Depending on the version of Word that you are using, look to the tabs at the top of your document. Most people never venture beyond the Home tab. Try the Review tab and to the left you should see Translate. While you are at it, click through all the tabs along the top of the document. You may discover great things you didn't know existed in Word. There are lots of options! Do beware that this translation tool actually sends your language out over the internet to be translated. You will get a pop-up warning you of that. If the language or document that you are translating is confidential in nature, this may not be the tool to use. Otherwise, it is quite convenient and will give you a good idea of what your document says.

So, now you are pretty sure that you have the correct document, but you need a more authoritative legal translation. There are legal translation services. These can be expensive and take lots of time. Preferably you'd like to find an authoritative legal translation that someone else has already paid for and is willing to share with you. Strategies for finding these…again, think of a professional organization that works with these laws all the time. Who will have these tools in their toolbox already? Think of government entities that would have official translations, maybe diplomatic branches of the government in question, or trade representatives. Search for those websites. Another great resource is law libraries. Law librarians are pretty much the same the world over. We may look a little different, or speak different languages. But deep down we love helping people find the information that they need. We will tell you we do it for you, but we're really just feeding our own addictions to information. Yes, we are those info junkies that your mother warned you about. Ask us a question and we won't be able to *not* answer it. It will keep us up at night until we find the answer. So, think of a law library in the country that you are researching. If the country has a law school or law schools that are online, this is a good place to start. Reach out to the people who work there. Tell them how great they are and how much you really appreciate their expertise. They are likely to have an official translation if one exists, or to know where you can get one. Really, we do get calls and emails from librarians in other countries all the time, asking just these types of questions. Also, if you know of an author from that country who writes on a specific topic, do some Googling to see if you can find contact information for that author and contact them directly. If you need help brainstorming ideas on where to find your document translated in a form that you can trust, reach out to your local law librarian for ideas. There are people out there. Just be persistent.

Chapter 8

International Law

Quick Start Page

The United Nations Treaty Collection has many authoritative treaty texts as well as the ever-important status information for those treaties.

https://treaties.un.org/

The American Society of International Law has good electronic resources including a database of international legal materials, organized according to subject matter, called the Electronic Information System for International Law (EISIL).

http://www.eisil.org/

For more in-depth research guidance from ASIL, try the Electronic Resource Guide (ERG).

http://www.asil.org/resources/electronic-resource-guide-erg

ASIL also offers Insights, which are articles on current topics in international law.

http://www.asil.org/insights

New York University's GlobaLex offers legal research guides for international law topics.

http://www.nyulawglobal.org/globalex/#

The World Legal Information Institute is always worth a look.

http://worldlii.org/

For more on international legal research, please keep reading...

International Law

We should probably start with some definitions, though those can be challenging with international law. If you read the chapter on foreign law, then you already know there is a difference, but also considerable overlap, between foreign and international law. Foreign law is simply the domestic law of a country where you are not. It sets out the relationship between the government and its citizens, or between citizens. It is confined to the political boundaries of that country. There are people who would disagree with that last statement, but that is a topic for an entirely different book. By contrast, international law is comprised of legal agreements that govern relationships between sovereign nation states. If we use the word state in this chapter, in this context we mean sovereign nation state. You will see the word state used this way throughout international law, so we will get you accustomed to seeing it here. The words international and transnational are often used interchangeably. To the extent that there is a distinction, transnational law deals with happenings that tend to cross national boundaries, or the effects of happenings that cross national boundaries. Supranational is another matter. Currently the European Union (E.U.) http://europa.eu/ is the only truly supranational entity that we have in the world. Member states actually surrender some sovereignty to join the E.U. In return, the E.U. acts as a governing body in certain subject areas with laws binding on the member states. We will talk more about the E.U. later in this chapter.

Before we get too much further along, we should discuss the forms that international law may take, so we know what types of documents we will be researching. Then we will move on to discuss great free online sources for those documents. Let's discuss treaties. Treaties are not to be confused with treatises. Treatises are books (or sets of books, or databases) that examine one legal subject in-depth. To read more about treatises, see the chapter on secondary sources. On the other hand, treaties are agreements between states or international organizations that are governed by international law. Treaties can be bilateral (between two parties) or multilateral (between multiple parties). Agreements between states need not be treaties if local law is intended to govern. For example, if one country wishes to lease a building within another country, that can be done simply by domestic lease agreement. Treaties can be called by many names including conventions, pacts, covenants, charters, protocols, and they can be constitutions of international organizations or tribunals. Treaties can regulate most things that domestic laws regulate, just on an international scale. We will look at sources for international law for many different subject areas. This book will only scratch the surface of all the great resources. If you need more information on sources for a particular subject, reach out to a law librarian.

The treaty making process can be quite interesting, particularly if you like politics and strategy. Because of the complexity, treaty practice can be slow and tedious, but there is plenty of work to do. If you think you are interested in treaty practice, we recommend that you consult the Vienna Convention on the Law of Treaties (often abbreviated V.C.L.T.) 1155 U.N.T.S. 331. http://legal.un.org/ilc/texts/instruments/english/conventions/1_1_1969.pdf You can also do a quick Google search (or your favorite search engine) for Vienna Convention on the Law Of Treaties, and find many good places to access it. Now that we have waded into the subject of international legal citations, the previous citation abbreviation stands for United Nations Treaty Series. This is one of many collections of treaties. For a good international citation guide, see New York University's Guide to Foreign and International Legal Citations. There is a new edition for sale. The first edition is available here in .pdf. http://www.law.nyu.edu/sites/default/files/upload_documents/Final_GFILC_pdf.pdf

Let's talk some more about treaty creation. Bilateral treaties can arise from diplomatic notes between the two countries involved. One country says, "We would like to do this." The other responds, "That sounds good, but we would like to include this." And so it goes, until they reach an agreement. For bilateral treaties, entry into force can be pretty much whenever an agreement is reached between the two nations. Multilateral treaties can be more involved. Very often there will be diplomatic conferences organized specifically for the purpose of drafting a multilateral treaty. Frequently those treaties come to be called by the name of the city where they were negotiated. Delegations from all the nations thought to be concerned are sent to the conference. These delegations may consist of diplomatic personnel and lawyers. Sometimes those are the same people. Frequently these conferences include not only discussion about the subject matter of the treaty but negotiations about the wording, in multiple languages, right from the beginning. It is much better to draft an agreement in all of the languages concerned, than to draft then translate, translate, translate. Entry into force requirements can also be included within the language of the agreement, as well as restrictions or requirements for parties wishing to join, processes for doing so, specifics about what constitutes breach of the agreement, and so on. Those people who draft treaties try to incorporate all aspects of the agreement throughout its life cycle. Because there is no way that anyone can possibly predict every last thing that might happen, it is also a good idea to make provisions within the treaty for amendments and also for dispute resolution.

Now that the treaty has been written, parties can signal their intent to be bound by signing the treaty. In the case of the United States, this falls to the Executive branch of the federal government, and this is only the first step for the United States. Signing a treaty does not make it "binding". Actually, enforcement is a whole different issue in international law. That is probably a topic for a different book. At any rate, the United States then requires the Executive branch to gain advice and consent of the Senate before a treaty is ratified, that is before the treaty is considered to be binding on the United States. Depending on which political party was in power when the treaty was signed, if the same party is in power when the treaty makes it through the Senate, and whether that party wants to spend the political capital necessary to get consent for the treaty… treaties can flounder for decades. Now multiply that by however many other nations were at the treaty drafting conference and all of their corresponding domestic processes. You begin to see the complexity of international law. While we are still at this stage, we want to mention that there are documents that can be found from the drafting conferences called *travaux preparatoires*, translated literally, preparatory works. These are much like domestic legislation's committee reports and staff analysis. They are the record of what was considered and amended and argued over. These documents can be a gold mine of information about the intent of the parties in drafting the agreement.

Also speaking of drafting, beware that this is an intensely political process. There will be nations who attend treaty drafting conferences and lobby heavily for particular language, without any intention of ever ratifying the treaty themselves. Again, if you like politics and strategy, treaty practice may be for you. Parties may also wish to sign a treaty "with reservations". Reservations are statements that change the legal meaning of the text of the treaty. Lawyers being how we are, we try to call them other things... understandings, declarations, or clarifications. "We understand this paragraph to mean X", when clearly it means Y. Or, "We just want to clarify that this paragraph means Blah blah blah" when it actually means yadda yadda. No matter what we call it, if it changes the legal meaning of the text, it is a reservation. It will be up to the other parties to the treaty whether they accept the reservation or not. The conditions under which reservations will be accepted should be addressed, to the extent possible, in the text of the treaty. The text of the treaty should also explain how and under what circumstances other nations can be added, if desirable, after the initial signing period. It has even been known to happen that new nations come into existence after treaties are in place, and want to join the group. If the group wants other states to join, they should explain the particulars of that process in the treaty itself... or at least make provision for how to amend the treaty. So, when unexpected happenings occur, like another country comes along who wants to join and we hadn't thought of that before, amendments can be made. It is all very similar to the process of domestic legislation drafting. It is a balance of leaving enough wiggle room that the document is workable, without leaving it so flexible as to be ultimately meaningless.

Now, the treaty has been negotiated, drafted, signed, ratified (with or without reservations), and it has entered into force. We arrive on the scene ready to do research. What do we need? We need the authoritative text of the treaty, and possibly an authoritative translation. We also need the status information: who signed the treaty, have they ratified it, did they do so with reservations, what were the reservations, were the reservations accepted, has the treaty entered into force... and oh yes, has there been breach of the terms of the treaty? Hopefully in our excellent drafting, we thought to spell out what constitutes breach and what that would mean to the non-breaching members of the agreement. Speaking of breach, there are a few basics of participating in treaties. Member states are expected to perform in good faith. The treaty that has been ratified is binding on the entire territory of the member state... no reserving one corner of your country where you can do whatever you want. Treaties also do not create rights or obligations for third parties without their consent. Just because you agreed, doesn't mean you can hold the whole world to the same standard. Also, treaties can govern between states on any subject matter as long as it doesn't contradict *jus cogens*, that is, concepts thought to be internationally accepted legal norms. So, no treaties are allowed for conducting slavery, or genocide, or the like. This is similar to domestic law. We can have a contract where I sell you my car. If we want that exchange to happen for $1, that is our business and no one will tell us that we can't do that. I cannot, however, sell you a car that I have stolen… nor can I sell you my children. For more on these concepts within international law, see the Vienna Convention on the Law of Treaties.

Finally, let's get to the good stuff. We know what we are looking for, but where do we find it? If you are starting with just a topic, you may want to start with a good secondary source. Secondary sources explain an area of the law, give you some context, and then point you to the primary documents. We really like the American Society of International Law's electronic resources. http://www.asil.org/resources/eresources (see Figure 8-1)

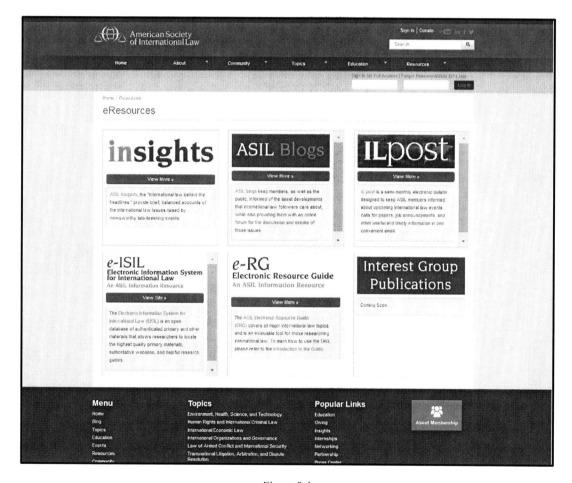

Figure 8-1

American Society of International Law

ASIL graciously provides these resources from their webpage. They include the Electronic Information System for International Law (EISIL). http://www.eisil.org/ EISIL is organized by subject for browsing. Because this is maintained by international law professionals, they understand that you need primary documents to be listed first. Under each subject you will find the negotiated documents from authoritative sources, then links to organizations or tribunals dealing with the subject, then legal research guides. If you know specifically what you are looking for and are not sure which subheading pertains, there is a search box at the top of the EISIL page. Conducting a search will bring back results from all across the database. For more in-depth guidance on researching an international law topic, ASIL also has the Electronic Resource Guide (ERG). http://www.asil.org/resources/electronic-resource-guide-erg The chapters of the ERG are interlinked with pages in EISIL so that you can easily navigate back and forth between the two resources. ASIL also publishes current event articles called Insights. http://www.asil.org/insights These articles can be very, well, insightful. One note of caution: as we are writing this book, the ASIL website is in the midst of transitioning to a new platform. This is probably true of many of the resources we mention in the book. That is one of the great things, as well as one of the terrible things, about online sources. They constantly change. If at any time you click a link, or search for a website, and you can't get to it, don't fret. Try another way or another source, and come back later. Also, if you find new sources, or have new links to old favorites... please share them with us! A couple of other strategies: if you are starting out with just a topic, try searching the internet for a guide. Search for "your topic legal research guide", and then use your powers of evaluation to choose from the search results. You may also want to try the United Nations Audiovisual Library. http://www.un.org/law/avl/ Or New York University's GlobaLex legal research guides. http://www.nyulawglobal.org/globalex/# The World Legal Information Institute is another place that you can search either by keyword, or for a specific item. http://worldlii.org/

If you know a particular treaty that you want, you may start with a different strategy. The United Nations Treaty Database is a great free resource for not just authoritative texts but also treaty status information. https://treaties.un.org/ You can search by popular name, official treaty title, participant (country name), or do a full text search. You can also browse. This is another place to get lost for an afternoon... wandering through all the myriad treaties that you never knew existed. "There's a treaty for that?!" Speaking of specific treaties, if you know the one that you're looking for, try Googling (or you favorite search engine) "Name of treaty secretariat". Often there is a secretariat, or administrative office, that does the daily business of the treaty. If that secretariat has a website, you are likely to find the authoritative text, status information, compliance reports, procedures and forms... all in one convenient place. Secretariat websites can save you lots of time. Party or member compliance information, frequently called country reports, can also be found at watchdog organization websites. We will talk more about that in a little while. You may also consider finding the treaty on the government website of one of the parties to the treaty. The United States Department of State, the diplomatic branch of the federal government, has a Treaty Affairs page. http://www.state.gov/s/l/treaty/ Here you can find a list of Treaties In Force. That is the title of the actual compilation. You can also find texts of treaties, treaties that are pending in the Senate, and links to other informative pages about how to conduct treaty research. Other government entities might be equally helpful. For example, try the Internal Revenue Service website for tax treaties. http://www.irs.gov/Individuals/International-Taxpayers/Tax-Treaties Or try the United States Trade Representative's Office for trade agreements. http://www.ustr.gov/trade-agreements This strategy goes back to our tip about thinking of who would have the information that you need and would be willing to share it. It also applies to other countries. Think of which government entity in another country would likely have treaty information and look there.

International organizations come in two basic types: inter-governmental organizations (IGOs) and non-governmental organizations (NGOs). They are just like they sound. IGOs have governments as members. NGOs do not act on behalf of governments. Both can be great sources of international legal information. Arguably, NGOs can be the source of more accurate, or less biased, information about country compliance in international agreements than the countries themselves. IGOs tend to be larger and cover multiple topics, where NGOs tend to be advocacy groups for specific issues. This is another one of our vast oversimplifications. Maybe some examples will help clarify. The United Nations http://www.un.org/ is an IGO, as is the World Trade Organization. http://www.wto.org/ Both have fabulous free online resources. Amnesty International https://www.amnesty.org/ and Doctors Without Borders (Medecins Sans Frontieres) http://www.doctorswithoutborders.org/ are NGOs. They also have great free online resources. The perspectives of these groups are completely different. For the remainder of this chapter we will run through a list of sources and the kinds of information they offer.

For international business, there are websites that run the spectrum of a business transaction lifecycle. For the contract phase of an international business deal, one of our two favorites is the Pace Law School CISG website. http://www.cisg.law.pace.edu/ CISG stands for Convention on the Contract for the International Sale of Goods. This great database includes treaty text and legislative history of the CISG, cases searchable by article of the CISG, commentaries, and if you scroll to the bottom of the page you can hear the CISG song by Prof. Flechtner. You know we are nerds when we like listening to songs about contracts for the international sale of goods. Our other favorite is UNCITRAL. http://www.uncitral.org/ That is the United Nations Commission on International Trade Law. This site offers UNCITRAL texts and status as well as library resources and a case law database called CLOUT, which stands for Case Law On UNCITRAL Texts. http://www.uncitral.org/uncitral/en/case_law.html Other resources that we like are the Organization for Economic Cooperation and Development, the OECD. http://www.oecd.org/ The World Trade Organization can be found at the following wesbite. http://www.wto.org/ The International Institute for the Unification of Private Law, UNIDROIT, can be found here http://www.unidroit.org and UNILEX, http://www.unilex.info/ is a database of international case law based on CISG and UNIDROIT Principles. Concerning the financing of international business deals, see the International Chamber of Commerce (ICC) http://www.iccwbo.org/ and the Society for Worldwide Interbank Financial Telecommunication (SWIFT) http://www.swift.com/index.page?lang=en . Also concerning economic development, visit these websites: The International Monetary Fund (IMF) http://www.imf.org/external/index.htm and the World Bank http://www.worldbank.org/ . Concerning technology transfers you may want to consult the World Intellectual Property

Organization (WIPO). http://www.wipo.int or the World Trade Organization http://www.wto.org/ , particularly the TRIPS page, trade related aspects of intellectual property rights. http://www.wto.org/english/tratop_e/trips_e/trips_e.htm Despite all of your best planning, if something goes wrong in your business deal and you need arbitration, you may want to consult UNCITRAL again at http://www.uncitral.org/ , The International Chamber of Commerce http://www.iccwbo.org/ , The International Centre for Investment Disputes (ICSID) https://icsid.worldbank.org/ which you will notice from the web address is affiliated with the World Bank, WIPO for intellectual property related arbitration http://www.wipo.int , the London Court of International Arbitration http://www.lcia.org/ or any number of regional arbitration centers.

For international criminal law research, we recommend ASIL's Electronic Information System for International Law www.eisil.org or Electronic Research Guide http://www.asil.org/resources/electronic-resource-guide-erg , and New York University's GlobaLex http://www.nyulawglobal.org/globalex/# . Other great places to visit are The United Nations Office on Drugs and Crime (UNODC) https://www.unodc.org/ and Interpol http://www.interpol.int/ . IMOLIN, at http://www.imolin.org/, is the International Money Laundering Information Network. FinCEN, the Financial Crimes Enforcement Network, is a similar service within the United States Department of the Treasury. http://www.fincen.gov/

For international environmental law information here are some great websites. ECOLex http://www.ecolex.org/start.php offers treaties, legislation, court cases, and literature all about environmental law. Be sure to click on the logos at the top of the page to link out to associated organizations. FAOLex is offered by the Food and Agriculture Organization of the United Nations. http://faolex.fao.org/ Be sure to try the advanced search options and to explore the links in the menu bar. The United Nations Environment Programme has a wonderful website too, where you can search or browse by topic. http://www.unep.org/ There are also environmental law advocacy groups such as Earth Justice http://earthjustice.org/ , The Center for International Environmental Law http://www.ciel.org/ , The International Union for the Conservation of Nature http://www.iucn.org/ , and Environmental Law Alliance Worldwide http://www.elaw.org/.

For international human rights research a good place to start is the United Nations High Commissioner for Human Rights (UNHCHR). http://www.ohchr.org Other helpful organizations that do work relating to human rights are the World Health Organization (WHO) http://www.who.int/en/ , the International Labour Organization http://www.ilo.org , the United Nations Children's Fund (UNICEF) http://www.unicef.org/ , United Nations Educational, Scientific, and Cultural Organization (UNESCO) http://en.unesco.org/ . Another wonderful place to find humanitarian law information is the website for the International Committee of the Red Cross (ICRC) http://www.icrc.org/eng/ and this is a good place to read the Geneva Conventions http://www.icrc.org/eng/war-and-law/treaties-customary-law/geneva-conventions/overview-geneva-conventions.htm . A couple of other advocacy groups that we have already mentioned are Amnesty International http://www.amnesty.org/en and Doctors Without Borders (Medecins Sans Frontieres) http://www.doctorswithoutborders.org/ .

Besides subject specific international organizations, there are also regional organizations. Consider that there may be resources available that pertain only to particular parts of the world. Not everything must come from the United Nations. You may want to explore the Organization of American States (OAS) http://www.oas.org , the African Union http://www.au.int/en/ , the Association of Southeast Asian Nations (ASEAN) http://www.aseansec.org/ , or regional groups with common goals like the North Atlantic Treaty Organization (NATO) http://www.nato.int/ .

We did say that we would revisit the European Union. It's not exactly an international organization. It is in fact a supranational government. Because it governs across many nations, it isn't domestic government either. The best analogy we can provide is the difference between state and federal government within the United States. Federal law overlays those of individual states, it doesn't replace them. States within the U.S. retain considerable sovereignty. Something similar occurs in the European Union. Again, we are guilty of vast over-simplification. Much more detailed information can be found on the European Union website. www.europa.eu For European Union law, see the database EurLex. http://new.eur-lex.europa.eu/homepage.html. You can also link to the national law databases of E.U. member nations from this EurLex page.

Remember that every source has bias, without exception. Bias is not necessarily bad, but it exists. Every source of information has its own viewpoint. It is your responsibility as the information consumer to think about what the bias may be and balance information from multiple sources for yourself.

Chapter 9

Other Types of Information

Quick Start Page

For general information, trust but verify using Wikipedia.

http://www.wikipedia.org/

For medical information good starting places are:

the Mayo Clinic

http://www.mayoclinic.org/

the National Library of Medicine

www.nlm.nih.gov

For business information, try the Securities and Exchange Commission (SEC).

http://www.sec.gov/

For general information on the Internet try the Internet Archive and to see old versions of websites, use the Archive's WayBack machine.

https://archive.org/

https://archive.org/web/

For lots more great resources on all kinds of topics, please read on…

Finding even more: other types of information that you might need in legal practice.

As lawyers, and librarians who work with and help other lawyers, we know that there are times when just looking up law doesn't cut it – you need more. You might be looking for medical information, or even information about a medical expert testifying for you (or the other side); you might need to find actuarial information, or company reports, or someone's address. In this age of constant social interactions on the internet, you might want to see what your client – or even more, the one on the other side of the case – has been up to!

We've put together some information here to help you with those searches for 'the other stuff', and we think you'll find some good stuff in this chapter!

Medical information

If you're doing personal injury practice, insurance defense, even criminal defense – well, practically any kind of legal practice! – you might eventually find that you need some information about a medical condition, a type of medication, side effects, psychological conditions, and more. There are lots of places to find this; the problem is that so much of it might be a bit dubious.

Let's take cancer information, for example. If you're representing a person who claims that a particular type of chemotherapy caused them to lose their sense of smell or taste, you might try beginning with a basic search engine query using a combination of those terms. And you'll no doubt find a lot of information regarding that – but much of it might be from persons who claim on their personal web sites that they lost their sense of smell – or didn't lose it. Or you might find someone selling a snake oil product that they claim avoids side effects from chemotherapy such as loss of the sense of smell and taste. Or you might find a web site of someone promoting alternative therapies, or remedies for those who can't sense smells, or....well, you get the picture.

The problem, then, is finding the best information that you can, and from reputable sources. Here are some sites we've found to be extremely reliable, easy to use, and thorough:

The National Library of Medicine http://www.nlm.nih.gov/, part of the National Institutes of Health, is a great starting point for reputable, reliable medical information. One of the reasons that it is so good for research is that it approaches the need for medical information from two different points of view – that of lay consumers, looking to find out in easily understandable terms what they need to know, and that of researchers who want a deeper understanding. NLM's home page, for example, contains a link just to "Health

Information" – but this Health Information contains everything from links to medical journal articles to a feature called "The Pillbox" that lets you identify particular medications by their characteristics. NLM also contains a search box, in the upper right hand corner of each page, that will pull together all of the information on its site regarding your particular query – everything from fact pages on physical conditions, to contraindications for drugs that might be prescribed for it, to outside links for groups that are devoted to that one particular condition. Basically, as a starting point for information, this may be the best.

The world-famous Mayo Clinic, in Rochester, MN, has a terrific web site at www.mayoclinic.org . While a visitor to the site may think at first that it only gives information about the Clinics themselves, look for the section entitled "Patient Care and Health Information". This area is designed more for lay persons looking for health advice, and can be a great source for lawyers trying to get medical information in a way that's easy to understand. For example, one section on "diseases and conditions" lets you look up a particular disease, to find out its causes, symptoms, treatments, even home remedies and prevention. While this site may not be the ultimate for a courtroom presentation, it provides extremely good information in a way that persons, such as client patients or jury members, can understand.

One of the best, handiest general medical books for so long has been the Merck Manual, well-known to medical professionals (especially nurses.) The many different Merck Manuals, including The Merck Manual of Diagnosis and Therapy, are available online for free at http://www.merckmanuals.com/ . These are extremely helpful books, with plenty of good, trustworthy information, and the online versions are very easy to use.

The Physicians' Desk Reference (PDR) has long been recognized as the authority on pharmaceutical information; its web site, www.pdr.net, contains much of the information that you would get from the book. While a site visitor has to be a medical professional to register for the site and get full access, much of the drug information is available here for free. Click on "drug information" on the home page to get to an alphabetical listing of medications; for each one, you'll find an extremely detailed and technical description of the drug, how it works, why it's prescribed, and its side-effects and contra-indications.

In contrast to the PDR, with its web site giving much information for free to users, is the American Psychological Associations' Diagnostic and Statistical Manual of Mental Disorders, the DSM-5. In law practice, particularly practice areas such as criminal defense, personal injury, or disability hearings, the DSM has routinely been used to identify psychological disorders which the client patient may have – or may be faking. The DSM-5, latest revision of the manual, is not available online to any great extent; its web site, at http://www.dsm5.org/Pages/Default.aspx , mainly tells how the latest version was written.

However, attorneys needing to use the DSM online do have some possible places to try. The main one, which surprises some people (not us, though – we use the site a lot!) is www.Wikipedia.org. Although it doesn't have the exact text of the DSM-5 in its entries for specific disorders, Wikipedia often has the DSM-5 code by which a disorder is classified, and a great deal of information about it. More importantly, though, are the external links Wikipedia has, some of which will lead you to other medical web sites which go over the DSM-5 standards and more about the disorder.

Gray's Anatomy – the standard anatomy text, not the television show – is not available in its entirety in a recent edition. However, if you trust that the human body hasn't changed much in the last 100 years (we don't think it has), you might want to look at the 1918 version of Gray's Anatomy, at http://www.bartleby.com/107/ (You can also find anatomical drawings and charts at the NLM and Mayo Clinic sites mentioned above.)

Business information

The whole concept of 'business information' is so large, and can encompass so much, that we'll just deal in general information here. The information that we've seen attorneys look for regarding business and financial matters usually involves company or product information (e.g., for products liability suits) and financial information. So let's look at what might be helpful in these areas:

The Securities and Exchange Commission has a database named EDGAR (for Electronic Data Gathering, Analysis, and Retrieval), an easily searchable system that gives access to more than 20 million company filings – almost any information required by the SEC can be found here. The main page for EDGAR can be found at http://www.sec.gov/edgar/searchedgar/companysearch.html (although you can always just go to www.sec.gov and look for the link to EDGAR.) EDGAR can be searched by ticker symbol, keyword, company name, etc.

Most every major company will have a presence on the internet and, for most of them, this is their place to keep investors in the know regarding the company's financial health and business news. A basic search engine query (we suggest using the company's name and the words 'official' and 'home page') should bring up the company's web site. Once there, look for information designed for investors or media; these are the best places to find out specifics such as corporate officers, physical address, parent company or subsidiaries, and more. Tip: look at the top of the home page, or at the bottom of it, for something like 'investor relations' or 'news releases.'

For your own personal financial interest, as well as information about companies you're following, one of the best sources for everyday information – trends, news, financial forecasts, etc. – is Yahoo! Finance. You can get to it directly from the main page. www.yahoo.com From the list of categories on the left or at the top pick 'finance'. Or go to www.finance.yahoo.com. Either way, you'll find a page with a large amount of information which is constantly updated. For the very latest on what is going on in the financial world, this site is among the best.

Looking for the registered agent for a particular company that you need to involve in a lawsuit? Or maybe a small business operating within a particular state? Most states will have a database that lets you search for corporate offices and agents within that particular state. For example, in Florida, the SunBiz database, http://www.sunbiz.org/ run by the Division of Corporations within the Florida Department of State, has this information. For most states, businesses are listed with their Departments of State as well, so locating that Department's web site will almost always take you to the official state corporate database. Our suggestion: use the "state listings" page at Cornell's LII site - http://www.law.cornell.edu/states/listing - to find the information for that state's corporations database.

What about those instances when a particular business apparently just doesn't want to be found – or its officers and directors don't want to be known? Most companies now seem to realize that customers and investors want to be able to contact them, but sometimes they haven't caught on. However, usually the customers have – and they're more than willing to share that information. So even if you can't find a phone number for corporate headquarters, use a search engine and type in a search for the company, using its name and the words *headquarters phone number*. This almost always works.

Internet Archive – for finding what's "no longer there..."

Among our very, very favorite web sites is one called, quite simply, The Internet Archive. With the motto "internet access to all knowledge", the Archive sets out to do just that, taking a massive amount of information and endeavoring to put some kind of order to it. It's a huge task, and they do it very well. And one of the most amazing things that they do is something called "The Wayback Machine". When you first go to www.archive.org , you'll see in the middle of the screen a very basic search box for the Wayback Machine, with no real details regarding what it does. But it's very simple: type in a URL (web address), and you'll get a timeline showing you on what dates that web site was preserved for posterity by the Internet Archive. Test it out: type *cnn.com* into the search box. You'll see blue circles covering most every date for the present year, but along the top of the screen, you'll see a timeline of other years. Click on *2001*; then on *September 11*. You'll see snapshots of the way the CNN web site looked throughout the day and night of 9/11/2001.

It's more than just an interesting web site, though. Of all of the non-legal web sites that the two of us have used in our years of research, this is one of the most valuable, because of the fact that it does have so much information that seems to no longer be accessible. Looking for a newspaper article that was published in 2006, but the newspaper's site doesn't have it? Checking on the employment history of someone who claims to have been a company officer years ago? Trying to find something that was on your law school's web site a long time ago and that you just can't find? The Wayback Machine is a gold mine for finding what seems to no longer exist.

Note, too, that the Wayback Machine does not just cover .com sites. During the federal government shutdown of 2013, many persons who needed to access government web sites found that the official sites were down – but the Internet Archive still had the operational versions of the sites from just before they went down.

Locating, and finding out about, other attorneys

Maybe you're trying to find out about an attorney representing the other party in the case, or researching the partners at a particular law firm, or need to locate someone in another state who can help get your cousin out of jail (hey, it happens…) There are several web sites that are good for looking up attorneys and finding out their background.

Martindale-Hubbell has been the standard reference work for over 140 years for locating lawyers, listing attorneys by city and giving some information about their educational background and specialty areas. Martindale now has a web site that also provides that information in a very easily accessible form. At www.martindale.com , you can search for an attorney by city, state, specialty area, or just by name. Even better – by using the *advanced search* feature, you can specify what law school you want someone from. So, e.g., if looking for an attorney in Florida who graduated from the University of Texas and does bankruptcy law, this could do it for you.

> **Quick tip**: The Martindale web site offers an advanced search option that lets you search for lawyers from a particular law school. This is not an option in the regular search box, and many users of the site may not be aware of it. It is a good example of why you want to always look for *advanced search* features; most good search engines, whether a large one like Yahoo! or an on-site search feature like Martindale's, will have some advanced features that can really surprise you!

Almost every bar association has a directory of its members, accessible to site visitors and searchable by name. For example, the Florida Bar's website has a link on the main page to "find a lawyer", which brings up a template to locate a lawyer. www.floridabar.org (see Figure 9-1) It brings up results which include the attorney's name and address, and sometimes more; many bar sites now offer attorneys the option of including a photo with their information. Most also provide information about bar membership, including the years of admittance and disciplinary history, if any. (see Figure 9-2)

Figure 9-1

The Florida Bar

A caveat here about bar sites, however: we've twice encountered sites of "bar associations" that actually are sites of anti-lawyer groups who have adopted a domain name similar to that of an official bar group. If you have a problem finding the bar association of a particular state, remember that the ALSO website has bar associations for each state, listed under "other resources" on that state's page. www.lawsource.com (see Figure 9-3)

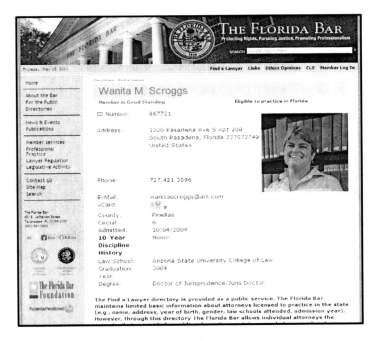

Figure 9-2

The Florida Bar

Other Florida Resources

1. **Government-Related Web Sites**

   Legislature   •   Browse

   See also the Florida Piper Resources list of sites.

   Additional Resources

   ¶ Vital Records — Contact Information ... [Elizabeth Orsay (Ind.)]
   ¶ Workers' Compensation — Agency Contact and Staff Contact Information ... [Robert W. McDowell / North Carolina Industrial Commission]

2. **Florida Bar**

   Appellate Practice Section   •   Browse

   These units of the Florida Bar have their own web sites, separate from the Florida Bar's web site.

3. **Bar Associations ♦ Law-Related Organizations**

   See also listings for voluntary bar associations on the Florida Bar web site.

   a. **Practice-Area Associations (Statewide and Regional)**

      American Academy of Matrimonial Lawyers (Florida Chapter)   •   Browse

   b. **Special-Interest Bar Associations (Statewide and Regional)**

      Caribbean Bar Association   •   Browse

   c. **Law-Related Organizations (Statewide and Regional)**

      Florida Academy of Professional Mediators   •   Browse

      See the National Federation of Paralegal Associations for links to websites of member organizations.

   d. **Local Bar Associations ♦ Local Law-Related Organizations**

      Brandon Bar Association   •   Browse

4. **Law Schools ♦ Admission to Practice ♦ Continuing Legal Education**

   Florida Bar—Continuing Legal Education   •   Browse

   a. **Consulate General of Mexico in Miami ♦** *Consulado General de México en Miami*
   b. **Consulate General of Mexico in Orlando ♦** *Consulado General de México en Orlando*

Legal Research and Assistance

Figure 9-3

Law Source, Inc.

If you already know the name of a particular attorney, you can try just doing a regular search engine query (e.g., on Google) for the name; if the person has a somewhat distinctive name, this may bring up just what you need. If you get too many results, though, and find it unmanageable, try adding something else. Try adding the word *attorney* or *lawyer*, or the city where the person may be practicing, or specialty area of law. Many attorneys now will have their own web pages for their firms, and many also have accounts on LinkedIn or other directories that will usually come up towards the top of your results.

Finding newspaper items

Newspapers can be a major source of information, whether pertaining to a person (such as an obituary or property transfer) or to an event (such as a news story about an accident). Most newspapers now have their own web sites, which are generally easy to locate by just using a regular search engine; type *Sumter South Carolina newspaper* into Yahoo! and you'll get a link to the Sumter Item's web site. And it seems that would be just about all you'd need to find the news – but sometimes, it isn't.

Many newspapers, seeing the internet as a huge source of competition (which it has been), have made news stories only partially accessible, some by requiring a subscription to read more than a few lines of a story, some by archiving their news stories within a few days and making their archives accessible only by – you guessed it – a subscription. (Note that many newspapers do put everything on the internet and keep the stories online – but many do not!)

As mentioned earlier, the Wayback Machine at www.archive.org can be used to retrieve items that were on a web site in the past, so if you know that a particular news story was published on October 12, 2009 in the St. Petersburg Times, you might be able to find it by accessing that paper's site for that date.

But what if you want to find older news stories and don't have a specific date, or only have a bit of information to go on? Here's where Google comes in, with its newspapers archive. Google has taken digitized versions of newspapers from throughout the world and made them searchable, some going back over 100 years. To access the Google newspapers, go to www.news.google.com/newspapers, where you'll see a listing of hundreds of newspapers; you can find a particular one by its name and search that, or just use the search box at the top of the page. Click on "search archive" to go through all newspapers, even the very old ones. (see Figure 9-4)

Quick tip: Newspapers, especially small-town ones and those from long ago, have lots of typos and creative ways of spelling names. Take this into account when searching, so, e.g., if trying to find news stories about someone named Ginsberg, try a search using the name Ginsburg too.

Figure 9-4

Google and the Google logo are registered trademarks of Google, Inc., used with permission.

Digging up the dirt: finding out about people

This topic is one that can get very complicated, and can seem more than a bit creepy to some people; however, it's also one that lawyers are doing more and more, and for good reason. Law practice is, for most attorneys, an adversarial experience; you have your client, and you and the client are going against someone else. If that other party has something about themselves out there that might work against them, you want to know about it – and more often than not, if there is something, it's on the internet. The trick is knowing just where to look, and how.

Just to be clear now: what we're talking about here isn't illegal or unethical activity, but using search engines and web sites to locate information about people. And although we could go on and on about this – with some really interesting illustrative stories about what people have found out! – we're going to just give some great web sites you might want to try, and some hints about how to find out more. One of the most amazing things that we've found, in looking for people on social media, is that many have no idea that what they put online can be found. Despite all the warnings, and news stories, and anecdotal evidence that internet searching can turn up embarrassing or harmful information, people still keep putting material out there.

A general rule: for almost every type of information you're seeking, there will be a web site, database or app to help you search it. Finding that particular system and learning how to use it effectively is the key. For many social media sites, these can change frequently; for example, www.youropenbook.org, formerly one of the best places for searching Facebook postings, has been taken down, but other sites will spring up to take its place.

It's worth your while to periodically look for sites that search the social media; you can do this with a basic Google (or other search engine) query such as *read Facebook postings*, and restrict your search by date, to find the latest information.

> **Quick tip:** On many search engines, you can do a date restriction as part of an advanced search, or using a command box on the left hand side of the screen. On Google, look on the page with your search results for "search tools", which will bring up possible time restrictions, including a year, a month, a week, a day, or an hour.

Some other things to keep in mind:

Don't rely too heavily on name/address/phone number sites that purport to tell you all the information about a person – many times, the information is outdated (we've seen information indicating that a person lives at home with a 92 year old father, when the father has been dead for over 25 years and the woman hasn't lived at home for over 30!) The same with property record sites, unless they are official state, county or city sites.

When looking for vital statistic information, such as birth records, date of marriage, date of death, or information about property owned, look for official sites. Look around the site a bit to evaluate it – when you're looking for information about a person's life, you want to be sure that the information is correct and that you have a good, reliable source.

Remember www.lawsource.com (ALSO) if trying to find vital records sites or sources; this usually will have information and/or links for each state.

Obituaries can be very good for finding out the names of family members, particularly persons whose names may have changed because of marriage (e.g., a daughter of the deceased may be listed with her married name). Among the free places you might want to check for these are online newspapers (and remember, you can use the Wayback Machine and/or Google Newspapers to get into archived news stories).

Here are some particular sites you might want to remember for searching for information posted by, or about, a person; these are the ones most likely to contain information not of a vital statistic nature, but more personal or social (e.g., social media, blogs, pictures, etc.) Again, please note that these are always subject to change – social media search sites come and go and change rather quickly!

www.boardreader.com – Boardreader is one of our favorite search sites, for the simple reason that many people who post on internet bulletin boards have no idea that those posts are searchable! This can make for extremely interesting reading. Bulletin boards – on sports, tv shows, colleges, weddings, diseases, weight loss, everything – can be found all over the internet, and this searches a very large number of them. Boardreader's default search is 3 months, though you can go back through one year of bulletin board posts.

www.social-searcher.com – Social Searcher purports to search 3 big social media sites – Facebook, Twitter and Google Plus – all at the same time; your results will come up, for all three, on the same page.

www.twitter.com/search – Twitter's search feature is terrific for finding real-time information – what someone is doing, or posting, at one particular time. Twitter 'tweets' will often contain Instagram photos as well. For finding out about what happened at a given time – or when something happened – Twitter can be an extremely good source, and the search feature can be used with someone's Twitter name, keyword, or hashtag (e.g., #legalresearch) that designates what the tweet is about.

www.icerocket.com – Besides searching Twitter and Facebook, this searches blogs as well, which can also be sources of interesting information.

www.youtube.com - We've been really surprised – though we probably shouldn't be – to hear about how many firms are now doing searches on YouTube. It appears that not only are many people doing things they shouldn't (such as faking injuries to get disability compensation), but some of them like to take videos that can be used against them - and post those on YouTube!

> **Quick tip**: What's a great search term to use, other than a person's name, when you're trying to find something on them? We've found that, in a large number of instances, a person will have the same user name for email, Facebook and other accounts. So, e.g., if you know the person's email address is salgwat@scram.com, try typing in *salgwat* and see what happens. We've also had luck using a combination of a person's initials and birth year, to find the user name that they would post under.

Keeping up with the law – as in b<u>lawgs</u>!

Much as we hate to admit it (life would be so much calmer if this weren't true!), things change all the time, and law is certainly no exception. New cases are decided, new laws are enacted, new lawsuits are filed, and on and on. There has to be some method to keep informed on what's going on in the legal world. Most lawyers will have some kind of current awareness tool, whether a bar journal, newsletter, or updated court opinions they check regularly. Another way of keeping current is with blawgs: law blogs, written by practitioners and professors, people with professional interest in keeping up – and keeping you up to date – with the latest developments in their areas of expertise.

You can find a very good directory of blawgs – searchable by topic area, among other factors – at www.abajournal.com/blawgs (the ABA Journal also publishes an annual Blawg 100, pointing out the best blawgs in several legal interest areas.) Another way to locate blawgs of interest is even easier – using your preferred search engine, do a search for your desired topic and add the word 'blawg' to it, as in *legal research blawg*.

So now that you've found some blawgs – and maybe even some other regularly updated web pages that you want to keep up with – you probably want to think about signing on with a news reader such as www.newsblur.com or www.feedly.com. (see Figure 9-5) What a news reader does, basically, is put all of your blawgs and web sites together in one organized list and update them regularly, so that each time you sign in to your news reader, the latest additions to your list are there, in one place, current and ready for your reading pleasure. Most news readers – and there are several of them – will also have search features for finding new blawgs and web sites on your interests.

Quoting Shakespeare (or Twain, or the Bible, or…)

We couldn't let go of this chapter without throwing in one of our favorite general-purpose web sites, good for so many things. Bartleby is the equivalent of an excellent shelf of reference works. www.bartleby.com True, these aren't the latest editions of the works, but as one of your authors once told a class in a monumental, yet pithy lapse into bad grammar, "Shakespeare ain't sayin' nothing new." Bartlett's Quotations is here in its entirety, as is the King James Bible, an older edition of Strunk & White's Elements of Style, and whole books of poetry. For finding eloquent statements to use in court or throw into a legal document, this is a truly wonderful web site.

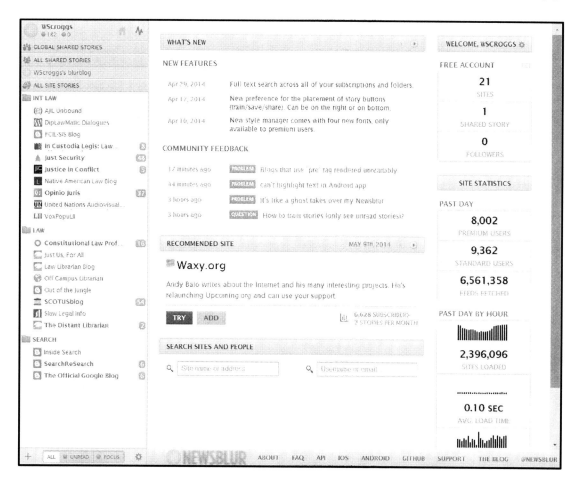

Figure 9-5

Newsblur.com

Chapter 10

Tips and Tricks

Quick Start Page

Use a good search engine, or better yet, more than one.

Take advantage of advanced search features.

Vary your search terms.

Check out links that are provided. But have a good anti-virus / anti-malware system in place before you do!

Critically evaluate your search results.

Remember you can use Ctrl + F to get a search box to search an entire document or webpage. Command + F if you're using a Mac.

Finding It:

Tips and tricks to help you become a better searcher

Throughout, we've given you a lot of information about different web sites and ways to find information for free. However, you're always likely to run up against an issue that isn't fully covered in those sources, or that you need more information to effectively work on. So much more is out there for you on the internet – you just have to know how to find it.

That's what this chapter is for: helping you to effectively, and efficiently, search for information. Some of these tips might apply to sites that we've already discussed, and some might apply to things that we've barely focused on yet, such as looking for factual information. So here, now, is what you need to know to become a good web searcher. Sometimes what you hope to find may not be out there – but follow these and, if it is on the internet, you're very likely to find it!

Basic computer tips

Some of these things you may already know, but some of them you might not be familiar with. They can save you time and get you to the good stuff a bit more quickly:

http:// - true confession time: it absolutely drives us crazy to see someone typing this in with a web address. You don't have to! True, it's only a few seconds of useless typing, but still, that adds up. Instead of typing in http://www.yahoo.com, type just www.yahoo.com and you'll go there. (You often don't need the www. part either, but since it can make a difference in some instances, we suggest keeping it anyway – and it's still fewer keystrokes than the http://!)

Using **Ctrl + F** – both keys at the same time – lets you find a particular word or phrase in the page currently on your screen. This can be extremely helpful when reading long cases or documents that have you scrolling down…down…down looking for one particular word. By holding down Ctrl + F, you'll make a search box pop up, one that lets you then specify what it is you're looking for. Try **Command + F** if you're a Mac user.

For example, if you were looking at the Jacobellis case, hoping to find the part where Justice Stewart says about pornography, "I know it when I see it", using Ctrl + F and the phrase *know it when I see it* would zoom you right to page 197 of the reporter version where the phrase is. Considering that the case begins on page 184 – 13 pages before – you've just cut out a lot of skimming that you would have had to do!

Another tip: the F3 key does the same thing, on both PCs and Apples. AND, if you're using the Safari browser, using the search box on the upper right of the screen offers the option to "search on this page", letting you search for a particular phrase or word on the page you're already reading.

One of our favorite discoveries in the past few years has been the **snipping tool** feature in Windows (the Apple equivalent is the grab command.) The snipping tool (its icon is a pair of scissors cutting within a red circle) is used to capture parts of what appears on your computer screen – instead of taking a screenshot of the whole thing, you can use the snipping tool to clip a particular part of the screen and then paste, edit, whatever you want (within copyright law, of course!)

Here's an example: if we were assembling a PowerPoint presentation on internet searching, we might want to talk about Google Scholar and where the buttons are to specify whether to search patents or case law. Taking a screenshot of the entire screen is more than we'd like. For our presentation, we want to zero in on those particular buttons. Instead, we click on the snipping tool icon, located on the Windows start bar, and specify that we want a new snip, and then draw a box around the part of that screen that we want. And here it is: (see Figure 10-1)

Figure 10-1

Google and the Google logo are registered trademarks of Google, Inc., used with permission.

The SALLY Rule: Your authors are not persons of great ego, and would never want to be thought of as such. Having said that, though, one of us (guess which...) came up with an acronym to help people remember the major parts that go into being a good searcher. And, since she came up with it, she got to name it. Here, then, are the elements of the SALLY rule – which we'll look at in much more detail.

- S – use a good search engine, and have another one to use as back-up or to find even more information
- A – use advanced search features
- L – language: what you type in is the most important part of your search and can make a huge difference with what you find
- L – links – look for them, even in not-very-helpful search results
- Y (pronounced as a long e) – yvaluate what you've found

Search engines – the most essential tools on the internet!

Even if you're not that savvy a searcher yet, you've still heard about some of the major search engines, whether Google, Bing, Yahoo, or maybe even some other ones. A good search engine can mean the difference between finding just what you want and finding nothing (or nothing useful). Here are some things to keep in mind:

First, remember that not even the best search engine is going to search everything. Think about how much information is available on the internet – things are being added to it every second, older things are being removed (as well as they can, anyway) or being moved to other pages, and no one search engine can find it all. So our suggestion is simple: find one that you really like, and trust, and feel very comfortable in using. And then find another one to serve as backup.

For many people, Google (www.google.com – very easy to remember!) is the go-to search engine, and for good reason: it searches through a huge number of web pages quickly, has great advanced search features (more on those soon), and has a nice, clean, uncluttered look that makes it very clear where you should type something. (see Figure 10-2)

But there are others as well, also reliable and easy to use, also likely to bring back good results. You may be a Bing user, or prefer Yahoo! or even AOL's search feature.

The interesting thing about the search engines is that, with almost every search you do, you'll get the same results....up to a point. And then you'll notice some significant differences in the results, differences that may be worth checking out. For example, articles that are in Google's digitized newspapers will show up in a Google search but possibly not in one done on Yahoo! using the very same search terms; a search done on Bing might bring up results that are specific to its own features, such as photos specifically on Microsoft sites. Both the Google and Bing searches will probably bring up the results from the biggest web sites, such as Wikipedia, but after that, results may vary.

Figure 10-2

Google and the Google logo are registered trademarks of Google, Inc., used with permission.

So pick two search engines, and use one enough so that you can be considered an expert (or almost) user of it – but have another to double-check or use to find more. Here are some suggestions for finding one or more search engines to use:

Try the big search engines – we've named a few here already – using a search that you know probably won't turn up much, just to see how the results differ from one search engine to the next. One of us will periodically do a search using her family name and hometown, to see if new information shows up on one search engine and not another.

One great web site to use to find which search engines are out there, and how well you like them, is www.seekfreak.com , a dual-framed tool that lets you compare the same search and its results from two different search engines, side by side. SeekFreak includes dozens of search engines, including many you've never heard of before, and the wide range of results that you'll see can be surprising.

New search engines are coming online all of the time, and others already there change continually as well. There are ways to try to keep up with this: www.searchenginewatch.com, for example, is a site that points out updates or features of different search engines, though at times it can be very technical. Our suggestion: every few weeks or months, try doing a search in several different ones, to see if there's a new one you'd like to keep as your 'spare', or even promote to being your new favorite search tool. Seekfreak can be a good tool for this.

Other search engines: Don't forget that even though you'll mainly be using search engines that search everything, almost every big web site, or even type of information, will have its own search engine. This means, e.g., that if you wanted to find out about a particular article in the ABA Journal, you could go to www.abajournal.com. Look for a search box, in the upper right hand corner for most sites, and type your search terms in there. This 'search on site' feature is extremely useful, since your search is restricted to what can be found on that exact web site that you're already visiting. You know that what you bring up will be something from the ABA Journal, not just a random web page from somewhere that happens to use your search terms.

Advanced search features – the difference between a good search and a great one!

Because there is so much information available on the internet, what you really hope to find – or something close to it – is probably out there, but it may be buried in a mass of material that has your words but is not relevant at all to what you need. Most of the time, you end up with too much information, though not of the kind that you especially want. Just as an example: let's say you're trying to find out what problems might have come up in cases before where jurors used social media, especially Twitter and Facebook, to communicate with the 'outside world' about the case. You run a basic Google search. (see Figure 10-3)

Figure 10-3

Google and the Google logo are registered trademarks of Google, Inc., used with permission.

This brings up several million (!) search results, many of them newspaper or blog stories detailing instances where a juror has been released or the trial affected. But you might want something a bit more than this, more authoritative or in-depth. Perhaps an author has done a study of juror attitudes on social media, or an article details the differences in juror problems 20 years ago and today, or a court has a handbook for jurors about what they can or can't do.

This is where the advanced search features come in. With advanced searching, you can use a variety of factors to narrow down your results to much more closely fit the type of information you want. Different search engines have different types of advanced search features, but many will let you define the date range of your results, or specify the file format, or look for information from a particular type of site. The best search engines – even those 'search on site' ones – will have some type of advanced search features available.

Advanced search features can sometimes be easily located; on the Martindale-Hubbell web site for example, you'll see a search box in the upper corner; underneath, you'll see 'advanced search', which brings up a template for more in-depth searching.

Google and Yahoo! each have very useful advanced search features, although they can be a bit hard to find – if you don't know where to look. With each, look for a round sprocket-like device on the upper right part of the screen; usually, this will come up with your results screen. Here, for example, is the Google sprocket as shown with the search results. (see Figure 10-4)

Figure 10-4

Google and the Google logo are registered trademarks of Google, Inc., used with permission.

Clicking on "advanced search" here will bring up a template with spaces for you to fill in as desired. You can pick among various restrictors and even combine some if needed; the idea is that you want to restrict until you're getting the best possible results.

Here are some of the possible choices for advanced search features on Google:

"find pages with...." – this section of the advanced search page offers options for phrasing your search. If you want to look for an exact phrase, you can put it in the box for that – and so on. Once you get familiar with the commands, though, you may be able to do this part without having to go to advanced search (e.g., you can just put an exact phrase in quotation marks for the same result.)

"site or domain" – here you can specify what type of source site you want your results from. For example, if you only want materials from government web sites, you can type *.gov* here. (Also, if you want materials from a site with a very large amount of information, such as the United Nations web site, you can type that in: *un.org* .) Again, if you want to do this without having to go to the advanced search area first, just include *site:* as part of your Google search, with no space after the colon, and the type of site.

"file type" – of all the many types of restrictions you can put on a search, this may very well be the best one. This is where you can specify what type of material you want. For example, are you looking for a good example of a PowerPoint on your topic? You can specify that you want PowerPoint presentations.

The most useful file type we've found, by far, is Adobe Acrobat pdf. Think of it this way: much of the really helpful material that you find on the web is material that's been published and scanned online or else electronically filed; this includes articles, court filings, newsletters, position papers, etc. Restricting the search for *juror using Facebook Twitter* to only .pdf files takes you to much better search results, bringing up articles and other items that take a more organized and law-oriented approach to the situation.

Note that Yahoo! has similar restrictions available for an advanced search. For Yahoo!, do your search first, then look for the sprocket on the upper right of the results page. Again, this will give the advanced search option, and once there, you'll have a template to fill in.

Language - you get what you ask for, so ask well!

Search language is always the hardest part of the search. The internet, unfortunately (well, maybe not...), is still not capable of reading your mind and figuring out just what it is you're looking for. You have to tell it. Since the only indication it has of what you want it to find is the wording that you use, you need to think carefully about the wording of your search request. And if you don't find what you need, think on it again, and rephrase the request. Here are some things to keep in mind. First, the more specific the terms you use, the more likely you are to find what you want – but if not, you're using the wrong terms. E.g., if you type in the docket number of a case you just know has to be on the internet, but it doesn't come up, look carefully at that number. Maybe you're missing an abbreviation that's part of it, maybe a number is out of sequence – but try it again another way.

Do a preliminary search, if needed, to see what terms of art, names, places, etc. might be involved; once you know more specific terms, do another search. Here's an example: recently, a student was looking for material about copyright and people putting their own material on YouTube. Those words didn't bring up much of relevance to what he wanted, but as he read a few of the results, one phrase appeared several times – 'user-generated content' or UGC. He went back to search again, using UGC as a term, and found what he needed.

Don't get too restrictive in your search – allow some wiggle room in case the item that you need doesn't say it exactly the way you would.

Putting an exact phrase in quotation marks is a great idea – up to the point where a court or author says that phrase in a different way. For example, if you're looking for a murder case involving Sally Waters, defendant, typing in "Sally Waters" will bring up cases where she's called that exactly – but you may miss cases where she's called Sally G. Waters, or Waters, Sally. The same applies to things like statute numbers, case names, even legal terminology. (Florida's statutes of limitations are in the statute books under 'limitation of actions'; doing a search in the statutes for "statute of limitations" might not give any references.) The wiggle can come in from just using your words without putting them in a phrase, e.g., *sally waters*, or *statute limitations tort* . If you can think of any way to state a phrase that might possibly be different from the way you would say it ordinarily – e.g., if a court might say "in Title 42, the section dealing with penalties, section 221, says….", then allow the wiggle room and put in *42 221 penalty section* instead.

Links – you might not get what you want, but see if the site can get you to it!

One of the really great things, among so many, of finding information on the internet is looking at the links to other information. Often you won't find just what you need, even using what seems like a wonderfully-phrased search on a good search engine. You might have come close, but not close enough! Even with those search results, though, it often can be extremely helpful to look at the web pages that have come up, and explore them for links to other information. Think of it this way: even when you've only found a law review article that mentions your topic in passing, there usually will be a footnote getting you to more information about it, and maybe more than one footnote. Those will lead you to more about your topic. Links work pretty much the same way, and finding and using them can take you to a lot of really good information.

One of our favorite examples of when links can be really handy is Wikipedia www.wikipedia.org. Wikipedia is sometimes frowned upon as a source because of the collaborative editing process the articles go through. However, if you look at Wikipedia for background, and the links that it gives you, you'll often find that it takes you to some really helpful information, and sometimes much, much more quickly than you would find it yourself.

Here's an example. Let's say you're handling a personal injury case that involves someone being injured while riding an escalator. You'll want to become familiar with escalator operations, and at least have a basic knowledge of them to begin your investigation of the facts. By typing the word 'escalator' in Wikipedia, you come up with an entry – a very long one – describing the different kinds of escalators, the parts involved, how they operate, major accidents and injuries that have happened, and more. Most of this is footnoted, and the information in those footnotes is hyperlinked, so that clicking on a link, you can find the information behind the Wikipedia entry. Following the footnotes, you'll have external links as well – links to sites outside of Wikipedia that cover things discussed in the article.

Is all of it reliable? With Wikipedia, we're fond of the Ronald Reagan adage, "Trust, but verify." The sources used on Wikipedia articles can be very good sources of information. Verify that they do indeed state what the articles say they did, and evaluate whether the linked site is a reputable one; if so, use the information from the original source, that Wikipedia linked you to!

Evaluate the information you've found - and where you found it

The information that you find on the internet can be wonderful – or not. The web sites where you find it can be trustworthy – or not. When you're using the internet as a source for your research, it's of the utmost importance that you have good, reliable information from a trustworthy source. Evaluate the sources of what you've found, to be sure that you can rely on them; once you have done that, then evaluate the information you've found to make sure that it's reliable and true. Much of this was covered in an earlier section, in more detail. Here are some things to keep in mind:

Look at the currency of the information. This can be extremely important in law, because of the constantly-changing nature of it. Don't just rely on the copyright date of a web page, since sometimes the design or information on a home page may not change, but the internal web pages might have later information.

For legal information, if possible, go to a court or government web site (.gov – and remember, you can use advanced features to get to these).

Look for a link somewhere on the web page for "about us", "who we are", or something similar. There should be something telling you who is behind the web site. If there isn't, and if you cannot find out who put up the information, ask yourself why they wouldn't want you to know, and look for it from somewhere else.

From our experiences in looking for information, it seems that most of the time when information is wrong, it isn't so much because of an attempt to deceive, but from a kind of laziness on the part of the person posting the information. An example of this is when someone provides their interpretation of a law or a case – make sure that you read that law or case yourself and verify for yourself that it actually says what the web site purports it to say! We've seen this several times when legal filings have cited very old cases that we suspect the attorneys haven't read, but have seen cited somewhere else.

Some more tips about finding good sites

Several of the web sites that we've used throughout this book are portal sites – they're designed to be gateways to other sites. The ALSO site www.lawsource.com and Cornell's LII www.law.cornell.edu both provide links to most every legal area that you might be interested in researching, whether by topic (Cornell is excellent with this) or jurisdiction. For the most part, when official sites, such as state legislatures, are available, they link directly to those sites; other links that they provide are almost always good, reliable and current (and we say almost simply because we haven't checked every single link on those two sites!)

Remember that, for almost every area of law, or legal topic, someone has probably already done research and compiled some sort of guide for finding information directly on that topic. Such a guide can be relatively easy to locate, simply by utilizing a good search engine and typing in your topic and *legal research guide*. For example, if you were researching adoption law in Montana and wanted to know what else besides cases and statutes might be available, type in *montana adoption legal research guide* to get links to agencies, libraries, and legal web sites with information about adoption in Montana.

A final tip: don't forget your library! Not necessarily just the one at your law firm – if it has one, that is – but many counties have law libraries, as do all law schools and many legal organizations. Many of those will have free access to databases, possibly even access to some pay ones; many will have librarians who will be more than happy to provide the information you need or at least tell you how to find it!

Index

CPSIA information can be obtained at www.ICGtesting.com
Printed in the USA
LVOW07s1223230814

400430LV00001B/3/P